THE IDEA OF WORLD

T0345610

THE ITALIAN LIST

Paolo Virno

THE IDEA OF WORLD

PUBLIC INTELLECT AND USE OF LIFE

TRANSLATED BY
LORENZO CHIESA

LONDON NEW YORK CALCUTTA

The Italian List
SERIES EDITOR: **Alberto Toscano**

Seagull Books, 2022

Originally published as *L'idea di mondo* by Paolo Virno
© Quodlibet Srl, 2015

English translation © Lorenzo Chiesa, 2022
First published in English translation by Seagull Books, 2022

ISBN 978 0 8574 2 989 6

British Library Cataloguing-in-Publication Data
A catalogue record for this book is available from the British Library.

Cover designed by Sunandini Banerjee, Seagull Books,
using a photograph by Adil Janbyrbayev (unsplash.com) on the spine.

Typeset by Seagull Books, Calcutta, India
Printed and bound in the USA by Integrated Books International

CONTENTS

NOTE TO THE NEW EXPANDED EDITION

The first two essays in this book, 'Mundanity' and 'Virtuosity and Revolution', were originally published in 1994 by Manifestolibri in a volume entitled *Mondanità. L'idea di 'mondo' tra esperienza sensibile e sfera pubblica*. These texts are wrapped around each other like conjoined twins: the original 'Foreword' printed below provides some information on their content and indissolubility. I propose them again with countless stylistic modifications that, without adding anything to the argument or taking away from it, aim at rendering my exposition clearer and more precise.

This new edition includes a third essay, 'The Use of Life', which was written in the summer of 2014. It resumes and elaborates on some of the themes discussed in the two previous essays, although from a different angle. But let there be no mistake: rather than a complement to the theoretical outline elaborated twenty years earlier, 'The Use of Life' is the stenographic enunciation, punctuated by peremptory theses, of a research programme yet to be realized. All the issues that are mentioned there—from the status of the pronoun 'we' to stage acting as a testing ground for the philosophy of language—would deserve some rigorous and courageous lunges. Far from drawing any conclusion, the final essay gets back into the game.

FOREWORD
(1994)

This book includes two essays. The first, which is plainly philosophical, begins with the examination of the states of mind that, according to Kant and Wittgenstein, pervade us when we think about the world as a whole, that is, the simple fact that it exists and we belong to it. For Kant, these thoughts are inseparable from the feeling of the sublime; for Wittgenstein, they go together with a wonder that cannot be subdued. But this is merely our point of departure. The first essay intends to sketch an idea of world that is not at all metaphysical, and, thus, able to enter into conflict with Kant's and Wittgenstein's positions—which are nonetheless adopted as a paradigmatic guide. Possibly, this—neither magniloquent nor sophisticated—idea should contribute to clarifying the implicit meaning of ordinary expressions such as 'the course of the world', 'worldly people', 'how to get by in this world'. On the other hand, the second essay, previously published in the journal *Luogo comune* in 1993, looks like a—minimal, of course—political treatise. It selects concepts and keywords (public intellect, multitude, intemperance, exodus, etc.) capable of confronting the magnetic storm that knocked out the compasses which, starting from the seventeenth century, had directed the reflection on the 'care of common affairs'. The objective here is to measure the perimeter of the field at stake in all its extension: with rudimentary tools, no doubt, but without eluding any of the crucial and ticklish problems posed today by collective action. This second text, I say it for the fanatics of gang wars, is also a reckoning with the work of Hannah Arendt.

The two essays are autonomous and can be read separately. However, from a conceptual standpoint, they imply each other like the words 'over' and 'under', or 'outside' and 'inside'. And they are also interlinked. Suffice it to think that the main theme of the second essay, 'Virtuosity and Revolution', is the notion of the public sphere, which is what the first, 'Mundanity', discusses in its conclusion. The point is rather that the two texts belong to markedly different, and even heterogeneous, literary genres. There is always a gap between philosophy and political theory, and incommensurability often prevails. This is a gap we need to exhibit without simulations. If we veil it, we successfully participate in the festival of futility: for example, by introducing a philosophical definition of 'politics', which does away with actual politics altogether. When we move from one level to the other, it is necessary to change language, premises, and units of measurement: the refusal to abide by this alteration only shows one's estrangement from logical investigations or proletarian uprising, and not infrequently from both. Those who write about politics must bring back the question of meaning and freedom (which is an ontological question for the philosopher) to the possible transformation of given states of affairs (which the same philosopher would specify with condescension as an ontic or factual question). Those who write about politics should therefore emulate the solicitude for empirical phenomena, operative procedures, and the variation of power relationships shown by Spinoza in the *Political Treatise*, when he dwells at length on the number and nature of the elected offices that it is appropriate to establish in a republic.

This book is dedicated to Anna and Elio, my parents.

MUNDANITY

SENSIBLE CONTEXT AND PUBLIC SPHERE

1.

Wonder and Safety

1.1 THE MIRACLE ACCORDING TO WITTGENSTEIN

In *Lecture on Ethics*, delivered in 1930 at the Heretics Society of Cambridge University, Wittgenstein affirms that 'ethics, if it is anything, is supernatural.'[1] Nothing about the meaning of life transpires from the propositions with which we describe the countless facts that happen in the world. However, each of us can recall experiences during which it seemed, at least for a moment, that we grasped this meaning (as well as understood what is 'irreproachable conduct' or the 'value of a man'). Without referring at all to spatiotemporal states of affairs, they should be considered as 'supernatural experiences'. But is such a mismatched oxymoron conceivable? Is a supernatural experience not perhaps tantamount to a *miracle*? In a certain sense, this is precisely the case: ethics is intimately related to the miracle. Provided that we rightly interpret the characteristic traits of the latter, Wittgenstein adds, so as to subtract it from the positivistic horizon in which the religious tradition itself mostly inscribes it.

---

[1] Ludwig Wittgenstein, *Lecture on Ethics* (Chichester: Wiley Blackwell, 2014), p. 32.

An authentic miracle is not a prodigious fact which subverts the laws of physics and deviates from psychological expectations. 'Take the case that one of you suddenly grew a lion's head and began to roar. Certainly that would be as extraordinary a thing as I can imagine. Now, whenever we should have recovered from our surprise, what I would suggest would be to fetch a doctor and have the case scientifically investigated, and, if it were not for hurting him, I would have him vivisected. And where would the miracle have got to?'[2] An event without precedents, whose imminence we could not predict, certainly astonishes us, but this is a temporary astonishment, doomed to fade away and vanish. Insofar as it happens *in* the world, even prodigy is nonetheless a *fact* liable to being described and analysed, about which we cannot rule out in principle a scientific explanation. It is pointless to look for an ethical meaning in what surprises and disconcerts us: 'For imagine whatever fact you may, it is not in itself miraculous in the absolute sense of that term.'[3]

In that case, what deserves the title of 'miracle'? According to Wittgenstein, the very existence of the world as the totality of real or possible facts is miraculous. More precisely, the experience of the miracle amounts to feeling *wonder* for this existence, to finding it extraordinary not so much *how* the world is, but *that* it is. What is here in question is inextinguishable wonder, from which we cannot recover. What happens to those who experience it, while they experience it? 'Wondering at the existence of the world' is the state of mind that attests to an impulse and, at the same time, to its failure: an impulse to look at the world from the outside (as a whole, indeed) in order to glimpse its meaning; a failure due to the limits of the visual field—the impossibility of picturing the field in which we are enclosed. If there were no impulse, or if it were fulfilled, in both cases, there would be no wonder. The latter emerges out of a clash

---

2 Wittgenstein, *Lecture on Ethics*, p. 52.
3 Wittgenstein, *Lecture on Ethics*, p. 52.

and is embedded in an *instructive frustration*. The miracle adumbrates what is unlimited, precisely and only through the perception of an insurmountable limit.

Wittgenstein subsequently mentions a second ethical, that is, supernatural, experience: 'What one might call the experience of feeling absolutely safe. I mean the state in which one says to oneself "I am safe, nothing can happen to me, whatever happens."'[4] What is miraculous is not the elimination of this or that imminent threat, but the certainty that no factual danger can compromise the meaning of our life (since this meaning does not depend on what occurs in the world). The feeling of absolute safety is the convex side, or the positive aspect, of proposition 6.52 from the *Tractatus Logico-Philosophicus*: 'We feel that even if *all possible* scientific questions be answered, the problems of life have still not been touched at all.'[5] Consequently, even if all scientific questions remained unanswered, and nature exerted upon us a boundless and terrifying power, what makes our life worth living would not be undermined or even affected. Not only is it sheltered but this is also the absolute shelter.

Like wonder, safety originates from establishing that there is a world. Yet there is a difference: the first state of mind arises from the useless attempt to represent the existence of the world; the second from the inclination to save oneself by correlating one's destiny with this miraculous existence, instead of with 'facts'. Wonder can always turn into safety, and vice versa: what lastingly protects us is only what lastingly astonishes us. Wittgenstein observes that ethical feelings, caused by the pure and simple existence of the world, manifest themselves allegorically in the common sayings of religion, especially in the most clichéd and naïve formulas. Wonder 'is, I believe, exactly what people were referring to when they said that God had created

4 Wittgenstein, *Lecture on Ethics*, p. 12.

5 Ludwig Wittgenstein, *Tractatus Logico-Philosophicus* (Abingdon: Routledge, 2010), p. 187.

the world; and the experience of absolute safety has been described by saying that we feel safe in the hands of God.'[6]

1.2 EXISTENCE OF THE WORLD, EXISTENCE OF LANGUAGE

Is an adequate linguistic account of the miracle possible? 'Now I am tempted to say that the right expression in language for the miracle of the existence of the world, though it is not any proposition *in* language, is the existence of language itself.'[7] Had we managed to represent our faculty of speech by means of words, we would have at our disposal appropriate terms to treat the world as a totality. But, according to Wittgenstein, this is precisely what is not possible: language is never able to account for itself. Therefore, 'all I have said by shifting the expression of the miraculous from an expression *by means* of language to the expression *by the existence* of language, all I have said is, again, that we cannot express what we want to express, and that all we say about the absolute miraculous remains nonsense.'[8]

If ethics is embedded in the cosmological question—not the question about *how* the world is, but about the fact *that* it is—this question in turn fully shares the structures and contradictions of linguistic self-reference (where what is at stake is not what we say, but the very fact of speaking). When we (vainly) attempt to assert something meaningful about the existence of the world, we are at the same time (and no less vainly) trying to pin down language, to portray it as a whole. Reciprocally, each and every self-reference has an immediate cosmological value; the infinite regression of the metalanguages attests to the useless impulse to look at the world from the outside. Equivalent and even interchangeable, these two orders of discourse throw light on each other in a negative way: each

---

6 Wittgenstein, *Lecture on Ethics*, p. 51.

7 Wittgenstein, *Lecture on Ethics*, p. 152.

8 Wittgenstein, *Lecture on Ethics*, p. 40.

offers an image (actually, the only clear image) of the other's failure. However, both the (meaningless) cosmological propositions and the (meaningless) meta-linguistic propositions always already presuppose that there is speech. In the end, the real miracle sparks when *we wonder at the existence of language itself.*

In a conversation, Friedrich Waismann once asked Wittgenstein: 'Is the existence of the world connected with what is ethical?' His reply was: 'Men have felt that there is a connection and they have expressed it thus: God the Father created the world, the Son of God (or *the Word* that comes from God) is that which is Ethical.'[9] Insofar as it makes possible every single enunciation, the existence of the Word (namely, the pure and simple having the faculty of language) duplicates the creation of the world, actualizing it again and again. Thanks to the Word, the event of creation is manifested in the life of mankind, for we are given the possibility to acknowledge a *reassuring* juncture between our destiny and the creator.

1.3 THE SUBLIME ACCORDING TO KANT

The experience of the miracle that Wittgenstein discusses in *Lecture on Ethics* is not different from the feeling of the sublime that Kant analyses in the *Critique of Judgment*. This is not a mere analogy, but an equivalence that can be ascertained in detail. The miracle and the sublime underlie the same state of mind, or, we may even say, sustain the same idea of the world.

Let us briefly recapitulate what we said about the phenomenon of the miracle so as to get ourselves ready for a change of scene. Wonder and safety usually pertain to the realm of facts: I am surprised by a colour; I am protected from an avalanche. What happens

---

9 Ludwig Wittgenstein, *Wittgenstein and the Vienna Circle: Conversations Recorded by Friedrich Waismann* (Brian McGuinnes ed.) (Oxford: Blackwell, 1979), pp. 117–18 (emphasis added).

when these intra-mundane feelings are referred to the very existence of the world, that is, to that which transcends facts? The meaning of 'wonder' and 'safety' is expanded beyond measure, adapted to a metaphorical use. But, for Wittgenstein, a metaphor is authentic only when it can be explained again 'in prose', by verifying its descriptive content.[10] Instead, expressions such as 'feeling *absolutely* safe' do not allow any translation: they are irreversible tropes, deprived of any literal equivalent. The expansion actually produces *nonsenses*. But the nonsense, thus obtained, is not nothing: its peculiar essence amounts to documenting a fundamental 'tendency in the human mind'.[11] Moreover, precisely insofar as they attest to the impossibility of representing 'what is higher' as a fact, pseudo-metaphors exhibit it in its transcendence (as it is thus truly 'higher'). This negative or by default exhibition, which avails itself of nonsense, is the miracle. Far from evading the limits of experience, the miracle arises precisely from the experience of the limit. Or better, it amounts to understanding the impasse as a *sign* (after all, in John's Gospel, the miracle is called *semeion*, not *teraton*, that is, 'sign', not 'prodigy').

Let us now approach Kant's reflection on the sublime in the plainest way, without avoiding some stereotypes. This feeling emerges from the inclination to grasp *in* nature an image of what lies outside nature; it merges with the effort to represent the transcendent ideas of reason intuitively. The sensible exhibition of the unconditioned seems to get a foothold in those empirical phenomena that make us think of nature as unlimited and omnipotent: 'the wide ocean, enraged by a storm',[12] if we decide to stick to a trite example. Yet the foothold does not bear such an onerous burden. The imagination extends itself tirelessly but in vain in the attempt to obtain a

---

10 Wittgenstein, *Wittgenstein and the Vienna Circle*, p. 12.

11 Wittgenstein, *Wittgenstein and the Vienna Circle*, p. 42.

12 Immanuel Kant, *Critique of the Power of Judgment* (Cambridge: Cambridge University Press, 2000), p. 129.

mundane aspect for what oversteps the world. Its progressive expansion only manages to *sensibly represent the catastrophe of representation*. Now, it is precisely such a catastrophe that determines the 'disposition of the mind' that alone can rightly be called sublime. Kant writes: 'What is properly sublime cannot be contained in any sensible form, but concerns only ideas of reason, which, though no presentation adequate to them is possible, are provoked and called to mind precisely by this inadequacy, which does allow of sensible presentation.'[13]

As was already the case with the miracle, what is in question here is a purely negative exhibition of 'what is higher'. The *expressive value of failure* is sublime (or miraculous). As soon as it unveils in its very productions the unbridgeable gap that separates it from the ideas of reason, the imagination 'makes almost intuitable the superiority' of these ideas. The verified insufficiency of any image constitutes the only possible 'image' of the unconditioned: it indeed *indicates* it as that which remains non-representable. In Wittgenstein's words, we can turn to God only by means of expressions whose nonsense highlights the fact that 'God does not reveal himself *in* the world.'[14]

However, in order not to miss the decisive point, the schema we have just outlined needs to be developed in a way that, to some extent, is also an actual correction. What goes beyond nature, but of which we nonetheless search an image *in* nature (contemplating the boundless desert or the stormy ocean), is nothing other than the *totality of nature*. It is the world as a whole that turns out to be unreachable for the imagination, in spite of the fact that the imagination extends infinitely by adding up or expanding mundane phenomena. It is only from this angle that we grasp the blunt formula with which Kant summarizes his argument: 'One can describe the sublime thus: an object (of nature) the representation of which determines the mind to think of *the unattainability of nature* as a

---

13 Kant, *Critique of the Power of Judgment*, p. 129.
14 Wittgenstein, *Tractatus* 6.432.

presentation of ideas.'[15] Given that it cannot be 'attained' by any image, the totality of sensible nature refers to something that transcends nature—it elicits the thought of the supersensible. We should not overlook the virtuous circle present in Kant's definition. What allows the presentation is identical with what is presented: unattainable nature is *already* supersensible, and the supersensible is *still* unattainable nature. The idea of world is embedded in this redoubling of the same kernel of experience.

The world is *both* the totality of the sensible context *and* the supersensible realm to which we are introduced solely by the 'unattainability' of totality. The idea of world is amphibious: redoubling itself, it always again guarantees the transit from this side to the other, from the finite to the unconditioned. Thanks to such a transit, Kant can conclude that 'nature [. . .] pal[es] into insignificance beside the ideas of reason.'[16] As adumbrated by the feeling of the sublime, *the idea of world authorizes and prepares the detachment from the world.* We will soon return to this self-destructive vocation. Before that, we need to examine more closely the complete convergence of the miracle and the sublime.

1.4 MAGNITUDE AND POWER

As we already know, in order to clarify the concept of miracle, Wittgenstein summons two different experiences. Wonder for the existence of the world concerns especially our faculty of knowing, or better, it takes residence near its limits. The certainty to be absolutely safe, 'whatever happens', concerns instead our practical destiny. This partition perfectly matches Kant's subdivision of the sublime into two fundamental kinds: *mathematical* and *dynamical*.

---

15 Kant, *Critique of the Power of Judgment*, p. 151 (emphasis added).
16 Kant, *Critique of the Power of Judgment*, p. 140.

The mathematical sublime, linked with the category of quantity, is the feeling caused by the *magnitude* of the world. Considered in its totality, nature 'is great beyond all comparison',[17] incommensurable with respect to the extension and duration of sensible phenomena. Kant observes that what is 'absolutely great' (*magnitudo*, not *quantitas*) is 'equal only to itself',[18] that is to say, it has in itself the only standard that is suitable to assess it. This means that the unit of measurement of an incomparable *magnitudo* is its sheer existence, or, as Kant puts it elsewhere, its 'absolute position'.[19] With regard to the 'immeasurability of nature' we realize the limitation of all our calculations, but, at the same time, we enter into a state of mind characterized by wonder and self-esteem that suggests to us, albeit only negatively, 'another, nonsensible standard, which has that very infinity under itself as a unit against which everything in nature is small.'[20] Now, the 'nonsensible standard' that alone can embrace the magnitude of the world is the very fact that the world *exists*. The further parameter, 'against which everything in nature is small', is the 'absolute position' of nature as a totality.

The dynamical sublime, linked with the category of modality, is the feeling caused by the *power* of the world. This is an irresistible power to which we are exposed without remedy as totally defenceless. In principle, we can do nothing to avert the threats of nature, the bludgeonings of chance, and pain. Yet, on some occasions we do not fear what is fearsome: if 'we see ourselves as safe',[21] we manage to contemplate a seaquake or a battle with detachment, and rise for a moment above the forces that usually keep us under control. The

---

17 Kant, *Critique of the Power of Judgment*, p. 132.

18 Kant, *Critique of the Power of Judgment*, pp. 133–4.

19 Immanuel Kant, *Theoretical Philosophy: 1755–1770* (Cambridge: Cambridge University Press, 1992).

20 Kant, *Critique of the Power of Judgment*, p. 145.

21 Kant, *Critique of the Power of Judgment*, p. 145.

state of mind we thus experience, in which utmost impotence and utmost mastery over oneself are mixed, reveals a non-contingent truth: the independence of the moral Self with respect to factual conditionings, its participation in a 'second supersensible nature' in which 'the dignity of humanity on our own person' is safeguarded from the pressures of the world.[22] Random safety is turned into absolute safety as soon as we discover a capacity for 'self-preservation of quite another kind than that which can be threatened and endangered by nature outside us'.[23]

Mathematical wonder and dynamical safety: magnitude that calls into question existence, and power that gives access to ethics. As we will see, the unity, or reciprocal interaction, of these two aspects is what constitutes the cornerstone of the idea of world. For the time being, the crucial issue is that the miracle and the sublime have one and the same articulation. For the sake of completeness, let us add that both the miracle and the sublime are familiar with *displeasure*, or better, with a kind of displeasure that contains its own antidote. The miraculous experience resembles a painful collision: 'My whole tendency [. . .] was to run against the boundaries of language. This running against the walls of our cage is perfectly, absolutely hopeless.'[24] And yet Wittgenstein concludes that 'the tendency, the running up against something, *indicates something*.'[25] The ruinous outcome of enunciation is in harmony with what we intended to enunciate; the clash brings with it relief. In the same way, for Kant, while there is certainly something 'repellent for the sensibility' in its dealing with the infinite ('which for sensibility is an abyss'), nonetheless, the obvious disproportion between the two itself turns out to be *commensurate* with the ideas of reason.[26] Hence, even though the sublime

---

22 Kant, *Critique of the Power of Judgment*, pp. 155–7.
23 Kant, *Critique of the Power of Judgment*, p. 145.
24 Wittgenstein, *Wittgenstein and the Vienna Circle*, p. 69.
25 Wittgenstein, *Wittgenstein and the Vienna Circle*, p. 69.

is a 'feeling of displeasure from the inadequacy of the imagination',[27] it still provides an ascetic satisfaction (a 'negative pleasure', Kant writes), given that it is precisely this inadequacy that stresses the transcendence of reason and, as it were, commends it.

1.5 ICONOCLASM

In *Lectures on Aesthetics*, Hegel shows the proximity, but also the gap, between the concept of the sublime and the ordinary notion of the miracle. His remarks enable us once again to establish at a glance Kant's and Wittgenstein's positions as well as their thorough consonance.

According to Hegel, the sublime expresses 'the sense of man's finitude and the insurmountable aloofness of God'.[28] In the fallen world, abandoned to itself, there is nothing that is capable of representing the 'positive essence' of the divine. The sublime is *iconoclastic*. It interdicts and belittles every kind of figural mediation. It reaches its climax in Jewish poetry, which 'puts the *one* substance explicitly apart as Lord of the world in contrast to whom there stands the entirety of his creatures'.[29] Kant already wrote that 'perhaps there is no more sublime passage in the Jewish Book of the Law than the commandment: "Thou shalt not make unto thyself any graven image, nor any likeness either of that which is in heaven."'[30] And we know that Wittgenstein continuously flags up the nonsense of the ethical and religious (pseudo) metaphors. Moreover, Hegel identifies the epicentre of the sublime precisely in the elementary observation that, for Wittgenstein, is the source of miraculous wonder:

---

26 Kant, *Critique of the Power of Judgment*, p. 148.

27 Kant, *Critique of the Power of Judgment*, p. 141.

28 Georg Wilhelm Friedrich Hegel, *Aesthetics: Lectures on Fine Art* (Oxford: Oxford University Press, 1975), p. 376.

29 Hegel, *Aesthetics*, p. 364.

30 Kant, *Critique of the Power of Judgment*, p. 156.

> God is the creator of the universe. This is the purest expres-
> sion of the sublime itself. [. . .] The Lord, the one substance,
> does proceed to manifestation, but the manner of creation
> is the purest, even bodiless, ethereal manifestation; it is the
> *word*, the manifestation of thought as the ideal power, and
> with its command that the existent shall be, the existent
> is immediately and actually brought into being in silent
> obedience.[31]

The word is therefore the only human connection with God's boundless creative power. But this connection amounts to the word as a
faculty, it does not at all amount to the images that the word forges
at each turn. And the word as a faculty—the very fact that we are
able to speak—is no less non-representable than the sublime event
par excellence, namely, creation. Wondering at the existence of the
world, therefore, is constantly converted into wondering at the
existence of language.

It is only when the feeling of the sublime has unravelled the infinite from the sensible world that something like a prodigious exception becomes thinkable. Hegel writes: 'For this outlook which can
grasp the natural course of events and assert the laws of nature,
miracle gets its place for the first time. [. . .] On a ground where an
intelligible connection is continually interrupted, where everything
is torn from its place and deranged, no miracle can tread.'[32] The sublime, with its pathos of distance and incommensurability, enables
us to appreciate 'that interruption of this accustomed connection
which is wrought by a higher power'.[33] And yet, Hegel specifies that
'miracles in this sense are not a strictly specific expression of sublimity':[34] in fact they present God's intervention in the world, while the

---

31 Hegel, *Aesthetics. Lectures on Fine Art*, pp. 373–4 (emphasis added).

32 Hegel, *Aesthetics*, p. 375.

33 Hegel, *Aesthetics*, p. 375.

34 Hegel, *Aesthetics*, p. 375.

sublime only makes us think of the irreducible disproportion between the two. But, as Wittgenstein would say, the prodigious facts for which we still lack an explanation are not authentic miracles *either*.

In Wittgenstein's interpretation, what is really miraculous is only that which Hegel ascribes to the sublime in order to distinguish it from the miracle-prodigy: 'The sublime in the strict sense we must look for, on the contrary, when *the whole created world appears entirely as finite, restricted*, not bearing or carrying itself, and for this reason can only be regarded as a glorifying accessory for the praise of God.'[35] In the *Tractatus*, the same point is expressed as follows: 'The feeling that the world is a limited whole is the mystical feeling.'[36] The mystical: that is, the miracle; that is, the sublime.

1.6 SUBLIME *TRACTATUS*

The connection we have examined so far does not fail to change our understanding of the individual parts that are being connected. The equivalence between the miracle and the sublime overflows in both Wittgenstein and Kant, throwing a different light on the questions they pose.

On the one hand, we have to acknowledge that the theme of the sublime is the leitmotif of the entire *Tractatus Logico-Philosophicus*, as well as the key that explains its rhetorical apparatus. Difficulties and equivocations arise from the fact that, in addition to analysing the genesis and peculiar logical structure of the sublime, this work is also an *example* of the sublime. It shows in its own itinerary the disproportion of which it speaks. The meaning of many statements made in the *Tractatus* changes significantly depending on whether we consider them as assertions that are as such sublime or assertions *about* the experience of the sublime in general.

---

35 Hegel, *Aesthetics*, p. 375 (emphasis added).
36 Wittgenstein, *Tractatus* 6.45.

Suffice it to think of the almost proverbial 'instruction for use' that concludes and, at the same time, disparages the entire exposition: 'My propositions are elucidatory in this way: he who understands me finally recognises them as senseless, when he has climbed out through them, on them, over them. (He must so to speak throw away the ladder, after he has climbed up on it.) He must surmount these propositions; then he sees the world rightly.'[37] Here Wittgenstein describes his book as a merely negative exhibition of the 'ideas of reason': it is thus a sublime book. But the *Tractatus* is, at the same time, a reflection on the impulse that drives us to incessantly renew this exhibition, as well as on the forms with which this exhibition takes place. From this second point of view, what matters most is not denouncing the inadequacy of representation, but the specific way in which this inadequacy must nevertheless be represented (*speaking* about what cannot be said, so that its ineffability becomes evident). Finding always anew a ladder to be thrown away after having climbed up on it is the fundamentally sublime experience. It is fundamental but also conclusive: only those who reproduce always again the *Tractatus*'s entire itinerary, having well perceived its senselessness, 'see the world rightly'.

On the other hand, we need to ascribe to Kant's 'Analytic of the Sublime' one of the traits that, according to the *Lecture on Ethics*, characterizes the miracle. We saw that Wittgenstein establishes an intimate relation between wondering at the world and wondering at language, that is, in short, between creation and the word: 'God the Father created the world, the Son of God (or the Word that comes from God) is that which is Ethical.'[38] For Kant, instead, the reference is to the *Old* Testament: he ignores the Son, and does not highlight the feeling of the sublime that accompanies the effort to intuitively represent language as a totality. However, it is easy to ascertain that

---

37 Wittgenstein, *Tractatus* 6.54.

38 Wittgenstein, *Wittgenstein and the Vienna Circle*, pp. 117–18.

the contrast between these faculties—that is, the insufficiency of the imagination with regard to reason—is in every aspect identical with the irreducible gap that separates *what we say* from *the fact that we speak*. Hence, the expansion of the imagination should also be understood as the vain attempt to express the existence of language through an infinite series of assertions.

Considered from a 'New Testament' perspective, the sublime refers to both Creation and the Word to the same extent; it sustains both the idea of world and the idea of language. Not only that: insofar as they are formally identical and reciprocally replaceable, the mundane sublime and the linguistic sublime can also intersect in a sort of chiasm. In this case, we access the thought of Creation through an empirical representation that rather belongs to the field of the Word, and vice versa. Otherwise said, the chiasm is articulated in the following way: *mundane* phenomena that refer negatively, through a manifest disproportion, to the *existence of language*; *linguistic* phenomena that refer negatively, through a manifest disproportion, to the *existence of the world*. For the time being, this crossbreeding between the two levels seems to be only a variation of little significance. But this is not the case. The chiasm is bound to play a decisive role as soon as we try to reformulate in an anti-metaphysical manner that 'unattainability of nature' (or of the Word) that constitutes the cornerstone of the idea of world (or, respectively, of the idea of language). It is then that the *oblique* version of the sublime, in turn modified in its form and content, turns out to be not only a possibility among others, but also the necessary step needed to think about the world without having to pay the price of a simultaneous overcoming of the world.

2.
The Emotional Root of Cosmology

2.1 THE UNCONDITIONED PRINCIPLE

The sublime is the emotional aspect of the cosmological ideas. Kant extensively discusses the latter in the 'Transcendental Dialectic' of the *Critique of Pure Reason*. The chapter on the concepts with which reason deludes itself into grasping 'the sum total of all phenomena (the world)'[1] follows the chapter devoted to the psychological idea (whose claim is to positively determine the pure Self), and precedes the examination of the ideas that target the supreme Being. The *cosmologia rationalis* lies in between the *psychologia rationalis* and the *theologia trascendentalis*. From a systematic standpoint, thinking about the world presupposes thinking about the Subject and prepares the thinking of God.

Although Kant locates all the ideas of reason on the same plane, considering all of them as an 'inevitable illusion'[2] or necessary errors, he does not fail to stress the trait that radically distinguishes the cosmological ones from the two other kinds of dialectical reasoning.

---

1 Immanuel Kant, *Critique of Pure Reason* (London: Macmillan, 1929), p. 323 (translation modified).

2 Kant, *Critique of Pure Reason*, p. 327.

While the psychological and theological ideas have at their disposal a specific transcendent object (the pure Subject or God), which is undoubtedly alien to any empirical experience, the idea of the world is only a 'mode in which we view the reality of [sensuous] objects'.[3] It does not pursue an unknown *quid*, but limits itself to looking at what is ordinary from a peculiar perspective. It does not yearn for the supernatural, and contents itself with conceiving phenomenal nature as a *totality*. While this instance appears to be concrete and realistic at first sight, it however turns out to be unfulfillable. The facts and states of affairs of the sensible world can never be known in their *entire* concatenation; they are never subjected to a *complete* synthesis. The totality of natural phenomena transcends every possible experience of nature.

> The cosmological ideas alone have the peculiarity that they can presuppose their object, and the empirical synthesis required for its concept, as being given. The question which arises out of these ideas refers only to the advance in this synthesis, that is, whether it should be carried so far as to contain absolute totality—such totality, since it cannot be given in any experience, being no longer empirical.[4]

It hardly needs to be mentioned that the characteristic traits of the metaphysical idea of world outlined here by Kant apply equally well to the metaphysical idea of language. The latter can itself be distinguished from the psychological and theological idea since it 'can presuppose its object as being given' (names, assertions, expressions of any kind); it itself consists solely of a certain way of looking at the habitual empirical phenomena; finally, it itself transcends these phenomena for the sheer fact of considering them as an 'absolute totality' (what eludes any linguistic expression is only language as a whole—the totality of possible linguistic expressions).

---

3 Kant, *Critique of Pure Reason*, p. 443.

4 Kant, *Critique of Pure Reason*, p. 432.

The cosmological ideas concern the nexus between condition and conditioned. While empirical knowledge goes back from the latter to the former, and then to the condition of the condition, and then, again, to the condition of the condition of the condition, infinitely, reason tries instead to put an end to this 'ascending regressive series' by indicating an absolutely *unconditioned* principle. According to Kant, the attempt to conclude the series of conditions, so as to be able to understand it in its completeness or totality, proceeds in four directions. Hence, there are four cosmological ideas. Kant divides them into two groups: while the first and second cosmological ideas have to do with the 'mathematical unconditioned'—the principles on which the 'composition of phenomena', both large and small, depends—the third and fourth are oriented towards a 'dynamical unconditioned'—the principles on which the very existence of mundane phenomena depends. It is worth mentioning the cosmological ideas one by one. The first: what is being thought about is the world in its entirety, and we ask whether it has a beginning in time and whether it is limited in space. The second: what is being thought about is the complete decomposition of a phenomenon, and we ask whether in the end we come up with something indivisible, that is, simple. The third: what is being thought about is the absolute totality of the origins of a given phenomenon, and we ask whether the phenomenon derives only from natural causes or also from a free causality. The fourth: what is being thought about is the set of conditions that makes a contingent existence possible, and we ask whether there is an 'absolutely necessary being' that accounts for it and sustains it.

The purpose of this cursory list is to accurately circumscribe the points of suture between the feeling of the sublime and the *cosmologia rationalis*. There is no doubt that the state of mind that dominates us when we face the incomparable *magnitude* of nature shares a lot with the thought of the entire duration of time and of the entire extension of space (that is, with the thought of time and space as the containers of all real things as connected). *The mathematical sublime is therefore related with the first cosmological idea.* Similarly, there is no doubt that the state of mind in which we taste a certain independence from nature is entwined with the always renewed attempt to go back from our contingent existence, threatened by imponderable dangers, to its necessary foundation. *The dynamical sublime is therefore related with the fourth cosmological idea.* Moreover, given that each of the two species of sublime corresponds to one or the other experience of the miracle evoked by Wittgenstein, we could also express things as follows: every time we pose an ideal limit to the 'ascending regressive series' of quantity, we feel wonder for the existence of the world; every time we conclude the 'ascending regressive series' of contingency, we feel absolutely safe. At this stage, we have fully unfolded the double constellation from which we took our cue and our material outline in the present pages. On the one hand, miraculous wonder, the mathematical sublime, and the first cosmological idea. On the other, miraculous safety, the dynamical sublime, and the fourth cosmological idea.

2.2 'THE UNATTAINABILITY OF NATURE'

The sublime is the emotional aspect of the cosmological ideas. But this aspect, far from being added to the idea like a makeup or a halo, is actually what allows its formation and determines its content. Therefore, instead of searching for the matrix of the sublime state of mind in the *cosmologia rationalis*, we should start from the former in order to decipher the actual meaning of the latter. Proposition 6.45 of the *Tractatus* states that 'the contemplation of the world *sub specie aeterni* is its contemplation as a limited whole. The feeling that the world is a limited whole is the mystical feeling.' The first sentence encapsulates the cosmological ideas; the second indicates the emotional aspect that is attached to them. Yet the 'feeling' is not a consequence of the 'contemplation', but its premise. We therefore need to invert the reading order: it is the feeling of the world as a limited whole, or totality, that causes its contemplation *sub specie aeterni*. Wittgenstein explicitly adopts this new sequence in *Lecture on Ethics*, so much so that, in there, the cosmological reflection amounts to the outcome of states of mind such as wonder and safety.

We already know that the feeling of the sublime arises when the imagination unsuccessfully comes to terms with the representation *in* nature of the *totality of nature* (as well as: the representation in language of the totality of language). What is initially in question is only the sensible taken as a whole; not the series of sensible objects and facts, but the sensible as a *context* in which every object and fact is inscribed. There is no adequate image of this context which Kant calls 'totality of nature'. Rather, it is evoked by contrast precisely by the obvious failure of any image we concoct with regard to it. In the first place, the idea of world is presented as the *'unattainability of nature'*. But at this point, a nature that cannot be attained appears to be something that exceeds nature. The totality of the sensible is only the narrow door through which we access the supersensible. The principle that completes the 'ascending regressive series' of empirical conditions is heterogeneous from this very series and incommensurable with it. In the second place, the idea of world is presented as *overcoming the world*.

This redoubling, produced by the feeling of the sublime, is the only content of the *cosmologia rationalis*. The unattainability of nature revolves around itself until it is converted into a departure from nature: the metaphysical doctrine of the world frees itself from that 'reality of sensuous objects' to which it is nonetheless exclusively applied. We saw that, unlike speculative conjectures on the soul and God, the cosmological ideas do not have a supernatural *quid* to which they apply, but solely consist of a special consideration of empirical phenomena. However, we can now fully grasp the meaning of this apparent modesty. A privilege underlies this privation: precisely because they are not bound to a specific transcendent object, the theme of cosmological ideas is *transcendence in general*. They thus constitute the ground on which every other 'dialectical reasoning' lies.

In the *Critique of Pure Reason*, the idea of world, separated from the state of mind that determines its genesis and structure, limits itself to complementing the *psychologia rationalis* and the *theologia trascendentalis*, or better, it is held between them. But as soon as we take into account this state of mind, every alignment becomes unviable. The feeling of the sublime assigns to the *cosmologia rationalis* an asymmetrical and primary position with regard to the other parts of the 'Transcendental Dialectic'. We need to emphasize two strictly related aspects of such an asymmetry.

We have just hinted at the first: given that it has transcendence in general as its 'object', the idea of world is the condition of possibility of the (psychological and theological) ideas that rather focus on a determined transcendent object; furthermore, it marks the access to the practical use of reason—the moral law. The thought of the soul and that of God not only presuppose the thought of nature as a totality, but, to a certain extent, they are also already included in it (suffice it to recall that in the third cosmological idea we postulate a free causality, and in the fourth an absolutely necessary being). There is then a second and decisive aspect of this issue: the idea of world gains a primary position and carries out a foundational role only because it is a spurious idea, deprived of any autonomous consistency, and exclusively employed to overcome itself. If it is referred to the sensible, the instance of totality involves the dissolution of its own field of application: 'Nature [. . .] pal[es] into insignificance beside the ideas of reason'.[5] What makes a strictly transcendent 'reasoning' possible is therefore the thought of a nature that is on the verge of extinction. Cosmology is of course a ground, but this is a radically negative ground (again, because it has transcendence in general as its only 'object'): it fulfils its task only by disintegrating itself.

---

5 Kant, *Critique of Pure Reason*, p. 140.

2.3 THE WORLD ON THE LAST DAY

The cornerstone of the metaphysical idea of world is the *end of the world*. The cosmological vision is always located at the point in time that concludes all time; it anticipates the Last Day in which nature, remaining 'rigid and as it were petrified',[6] will show the unalterable completeness that pertains to what is by then dismissed and overcome. It is only from the perspective of its depletion that the universe can be conceived in accordance with proposition 6.45 of the *Tractatus*, namely, as a 'limited whole', that is to say, '*sub specie aeterni*'. It is only with the apocalyptic interruption of becoming that the 'unconditioned condition' is manifested—that is, the condition that the infinite regression characterizing the enquiry into the connection of empirical phenomena tends towards.

Kant makes explicit the anti-mundane inspiration of the idea of world in a short text of 1794, significantly entitled *The End of All Things*. Why, Kant asks, do we feel the urge to look at the world from the standpoint of its end, that is, as an 'absolute whole'? Why, we could add, do we need the cosmological ideas? Kant's answer is: 'Reason says to [man] that the duration of the world has worth only insofar as the rational beings in it conform to the final end of their existence; if, however, this is not supposed to be achieved, then creation itself appears purposeless to them, like a play having no resolution.'[7] The idea of the end of the world (or that of the world as a complete totality, which is the same thing) is a witness to the fact that, as moral beings, we have a 'supersensible destination', independent from the course of mundane events. To put it differently, as Wittgenstein did in proposition 6.41 of the *Tractatus*, this (cosmological and, hence, apocalyptic) idea suggests that 'the sense of the world must lie outside the world. In the world everything is as it is and happens as it does happen. In it there is no value—and if there were, it would be of no value.'

---

6 Immanuel Kant, *Religion and Rational Theology* (Cambridge: Cambridge University Press, 2001), p. 227.

7 Kant, *Religion and Rational Theology*, p. 224.

The passage from time to eternity—which both the dying man and the sinking cosmos of the Last Day face—is, according to Kant, a 'frighteningly sublime [thought]'.[8] It has in itself 'something horrifying [. . .] yet there is something attractive there too';[9] something horrifying, since 'we come up against the *end of all things* as temporal beings and as objects of possible experience';[10] something attractive, since 'in the moral order of ends, [it] is at the same time the beginning of a duration of just those same beings as supersensible.'[11] As always happens with the sublime, we are, even in this case, facing an obvious discrepancy: the thought of the world coming to an end turns out to be inadequate to the thought of eternity; the 'end of all things' exhibits in a merely negative way a 'duration wholly incomparable with time'.[12] But here the discrepancy does not concern any longer the relation between the imagination and reason, but rather the relation between the different kinds of 'dialectical reasoning'. The cosmological-apocalyptic ideas are disproportionately big with respect to mundane phenomena, yet also disproportionately *small* with respect to the ideas that focus on the immortal soul and God.

A sublime raised to the power of two is thus delineated. Elicited as a repercussion by the inability of the imagination to represent it, the thought of the universe as a 'limited whole' elicits in turn, but only negatively (in virtue of its own insufficiency), the thought of autonomous transcendent objects (the soul and God). In addition to constituting the source and framework of the idea of world, the feeling of the sublime also determines the (negative and disproportionately small) relation that it maintains with the other ideas of reason.

---

8 Kant, *Religion and Rational Theology*, p. 221.

9 Kant, *Religion and Rational Theology*, p. 221.

10 Kant, *Religion and Rational Theology*, p. 221.

11 Kant, *Religion and Rational Theology*, p. 221.

12 Kant, *Religion and Rational Theology*, p. 221.

2.4 TOTALITY OR CONTEXT?

The world is, at the same time, too much and too little; *too much* for the imagination, which can never reach it; *too little* for reason, which understands it only as a negative connection with the psychological and theological ideas. We now need to interpret this 'too much' in a way that no longer involves the 'too little' (as instead happens in Kant and Wittgenstein), but rather excludes it. In other words, if, in the metaphysical schema, 'the unattainability of nature' is only the secular premise for the overcoming of nature, here, on the contrary, I would like to explain such an 'unattainability'—the unquestionable excess of the sensible context over the set of phenomena that are inscribed in it—on the basis of a conceptual constellation that interdicts from the outset its transcendent redoubling. As we will see, the first step we need to take is separating the notion of *context* from the aspiration for *totality*, and showing that the contextual *excess* is irreconcilable with, or even opposed to, the *completeness* characterizing an 'absolute whole'. It is precisely the assimilation of the 'context' by the 'totality' that makes the idea of world have as its sole content the overcoming of the world.

How can we secure a shelter when facing the threatening contingency of events? How can we interrupt infinite regression so as to be able to recognize and safeguard the meaning of our existence? It goes without saying that the materialist reformulation of the idea of world should not elude these vital problems, but organize them in a different manner. To this aim, it is necessary to define anew the experiences that merge, respectively, into the *mathematical sublime* (or the wonder for the existence of the world) and the *dynamical sublime* (or the feeling of absolute safety). But we know that the sublime is the emotional aspect on which cosmological ideas hinge; hence, discussing this aspect by following a new thread also means, at the same time, considering these ideas with different eyes.

Our further investigation of the mathematical sublime has the following milestones: the correlation between boredom and infinite regression; the analysis of the sensible as a pure context; the modality of possibility; the chiasm between language and the world. On the other hand, the examination of the dynamical sublime is articulated around the following fundamental themes: the dialectic of fear and protection; the uncanny as an ethical category; the childlike state of mind of repetition or 'Do it again!'; the intellect as common good; the concept of public sphere.

3.
Raw Nature

3.1 BOREDOM AND HAPPINESS

The mathematical sublime is the feeling that accompanies *infinite regression* in all its forms. These manifold forms can be brought back to two main species: cosmological and linguistic regression. Therefore, what is mathematically sublime is the vertigo and yearning that seize us when we search in vain for a measure capable of assessing the incommensurable magnitude of the world *or* of language. The imagination succumbs to the advancement towards the 'immensely large, with worlds upon worlds [. . .] into boundless times'.[1] Similarly, the imagination succumbs when, wishing to account for the very fact that we speak, it gets caught in the ascending hierarchy of the metalanguages (each of which always presupposes yet another metalanguage of a higher degree, in an interminable backwards flight). Kant states that the ideas of reason are 'provoked and called to mind' by the inadequacy of representation, provided that such an inadequacy 'does allow of sensible representation'.[2] Insofar as it offers

---

[1] Immanuel Kant, *Critique of Practical Reason* (Indianapolis: Hackett, 2002), p. 203.

an image of the deficiency of every possible image, infinite regression is the only occasion on which we are enabled to *represent the inadequacy of representation*. Therefore, this regression alone provokes and calls to mind the idea of world or that of language. It alone deserves to be considered sublime.

In *The Science of Logic* (Book 1, Section 2, 'Quantity'), Hegel devotes a note to the crucial intimacy between the mathematical sublime and 'bad infinity' (shortly afterwards, in another note, he dwells with perfect consistency on Kant's first cosmological idea). Hegel writes that:

> [...] the bad infinity, especially in the form of the quantitative progress [but also of regression] to infinity—this uninterrupted flitting over limits which it is powerless to sublate, and the perpetual falling back into them—is commonly held to be something sublime and a kind of divine service [. . .] In fact, however, this modern sublimity does not enhance the object, which rather takes flight from it, but bloats the subject who ingests such vast quantities. The poverty of such an irreducibly subjective step by step elevation on the ladder of the quantitative is betrayed by the admission that in that vain labour there is no getting closer to the infinite goal.[3]

Flitting over limits, without, however, sublating them, and instead perpetually falling back into them; what is the ultimate cause of this Sisyphean task, of which 'modern sublimity' is proud? A sort of melancholic paradox, according to which salvation is closely bound to the persistence of illness. In other words, the idea (of world or language), towards which regression tends as its *completion*, is exhibited only by the *uncompletability* of the regressive series; the backward march makes us think what would stop it only if it never stops. We

---

2 Kant, *Critique of the Power of Judgment*, p. 129.

3 Georg Wilhelm Friedrich Hegel, *The Science of Logic* (George di Giovanni ed. and trans.) (Cambridge: Cambridge University Press, 2010), pp. 192–3.

thus obtain a petrified movement, or a rapid paralysis, whose prerogative is to foment an invincible sensation of tedium.

The mathematical sublime is unfailingly correlated with *boredom*. The fact that 'a limit disappears, comes up again, and again disappears'[4] involves a monotonous repetition, from which the very possibility of an unexpected event is banned. The miraculous wonder for the existence of the world (or of language) is poles apart from surprise, and instead similar to the oppressive state of mind we experience when dealing with a tautology reiterated a thousand times. Infinite regression is, at the same time, the cause and the logical form of boredom. Uselessly striving to attain a comprehensive vision of the world and of language, infinite regression hollows experience out—it distances and distracts us from concrete mundane or linguistic phenomena. This false movement, which overcomes the limit only to confirm it, generates a profound *indifference* (if not vexed annoyance) for everything that happens and everything that is said. Sensible states of affairs and content-determined assertions slip away, without us recognizing their autonomous importance, since they figure only as random pretexts for climbing up a further step of the hierarchy of the cosmological points of view or, respectively, of that of metalanguages. When only elaborating a new 'discourse on discourse' and finding a further 'condition of condition' matter, an impatient lack of interest surrounds every single discourse and fact.

According to Giacomo Leopardi, infinite regression keeps us constantly *on hold*, 'without action, without movement, without warmth, and almost without pain'.[5] Showing the 'nothingness of all things', infinite regression creates a void around itself. It is precisely in this void that boredom—which is sometimes compared with haze or impalpable fog—seems to reside; Leopardi writes that 'boredom

---

4 Hegel, *The Science of Logic*, p. 193.

5 Giacomo Leopardi, *Zibaldone* (M. Caesar and F. D'Intino eds) (New York: Farrar, Strauss and Giroux, 2013), p. 114.

is like the air, which fills all the gaps left by other objects, and hastens immediately to take the place that they have vacated.'[6]

However, according to the author of *Zibaldone*, tedium is not equivalent to the absence of passions, but, instead, is itself the predominant passion, which is so radical and pervasive that we often overlook it. More precisely, 'boredom is the desire for happiness left, so to speak, pure':[7] it is neither hindered nor satisfied; it is even devoid of an object on which to focus. A desire for happiness—for an irrevocable fulfilment—is equally felt in infinite regression. What happens to such a desire? Happiness itself seems to have 'the same nature as the air'; it does not coalesce into facts or words, but concerns their connective texture, atmosphere, and *context*. And yet boredom and infinite regression (that is, boredom *as* regression) articulate the contextual or atmospheric character of happiness with a paroxysmal excess of zeal; they *oppose* the context to the facts and words that, time after time, occupy it; they devalue and negate them in its name. In this way, the 'pure' desire for happiness is soon reversed into the 'vivid sense of the nothingness of all things'.[8] But at the moment when the connective texture has no longer anything to connect, it itself falls apart and vanishes. In the end, boredom and infinite regression destroy precisely the context which they seemed to cling on to. Or better, they reduce it to an ungraspable *presupposition*; the context takes the spectral shape of an always-prior metalanguage, and of an even more determinant cosmological condition. Boredom and regression rarefy the very atmosphere of our life, the atmosphere that alone could have taken the colour of happiness.

The mathematical sublime originates from the vain impulse to portray the whole magnitude of the world or of language. This is the feeling of infinite regression. The latter's unvarying repetitiveness

---

6 Leopardi, *Zibaldone*, p. 1522.

7 Leopardi, *Zibaldone*, p. 1522.

8 Leopardi, *Zibaldone*, p. 114.

keeps us on hold and makes us indifferent. It bores us. The mathematical sublime (or miraculous wonder), with its monotonous vertigo, is never free from tedium. However, infinite regression is not an original phenomenon, facing which our enquiry must stop. It is only a peculiar and questionable articulation of ways of beings that are otherwise fundamental. We should now specify the *experience of the world* of which cosmological regression constitutes a specific twist. In the second place, we will have to hint at the *experience of language*, the meta-linguistic regression of which offers a deformed and partial image. It is only following this path that we can approach again, from a different angle, the problem posed by a 'desire for happiness left, so to speak, pure'.

3.2 SENSIBLE CONTEXT

With regard to the mathematical sublime, Kant speaks several times of a 'raw nature', to be considered merely as 'contain[ing] a magnitude'.[9] Unlike the beautiful, which concerns the form of the object that 'consists in limitation',[10] the sublime presupposes the absence of form, limitlessness, and chaos. This well-known and even trite aspect nonetheless deserves special attention. For Kant, raw states of affairs are characterized by little or no articulation: an overcast sky; a glacier without footholds; an expanse of sand. Formlessness is therefore a predicate that applies only to a circumscribed part of sensible reality. However, it seems reasonable to attribute another more demanding meaning to the expression 'raw nature'. Here, what we mean by it is a *mode of manifestation* of nature in general. What is at stake is not a group of particular objects (the ocean, the desert, etc.) but the potential *appearance* of any object. Every natural phenomenon, although it may be thoroughly articulated and even 'beautiful', can always be presented, on certain conditions and according to a certain aspect, as

---

9 Kant, *Critique of the Power of Judgment*, p. 136.
10 Kant, *Critique of the Power of Judgment*, p. 128.

something amorphous and undetermined. In this sense, the absence of form is not a mere deficiency, but a fundamental characteristic of the whole sensible world; or better, of the sensible *insofar as* it configures the world.

First of all, let us ask how and when sensible being appears as *raw being*. The starting point is the peculiar alteration of vision that the feeling of the sublime brings with it. This feeling affects, so to speak, the very functioning of the optic nerve, abolishing the *middle distance* and, consequently, perspective. What disappears is the *landscape*, with its highlighted details, picturesque proportions, and vanishing points. Nature withdraws to the horizon or runs into us; it is the inclusive background, or the immediately surrounding—tangible more than visible—matter in which we are always sunk. What remains is only what fades away in the extreme distance, or what, closely looming over us, expands into an indiscernible amalgamation. Departing from Kant, we could state that, rather than drawing on formless natural objects, the sublime state of mind amounts to the privileged occasion on which nature as a whole is manifested as *amorphous nature*.

This occasion is privileged but not unique. In fact, the sublime limits itself to extrapolating and exhibiting in a particularly clear way an aspect present in every perceptual experience, even the most modest. It emotionally highlights a specific task of the sensory apparatus—an unavoidable but also apparently secondary or interstitial task. The middle distance is lost in the *glance* [*nel colpo d'occhio*], where the gaze does not dwell on a defined entity, but has as its object only the visual field as such, in its entire yet nebulous extension. But the middle distance withers away especially when we look at things out of the corner of our eye [*con la coda dell'occhio*], that is, when we look awry or laterally. What is assembled at the edges of vision is neither perspectival nor panoramic, but confined to the background, or so close to us that it pertains to the sense of touch. It is either too far or too proximate and cannot in any case be put into focus; indeed, it amounts to 'raw nature'. But since there is a liminal region, or an opaque edge, in every kind of vision, a part of visible being always remains amorphous, unprocessed by representation, and indivisible.

However, we would be mistaken to believe that the formlessness of nature depends on certain physiological prerogatives of the senses. On the contrary, looking out of the corner of one's eye can become a relevant phenomenon, even connected with a *state of mind*, only because nature is always already formless in relation to our existence. Looking awry is not arbitrary or 'subjective'—it goes beyond the limits of a psychology of vision. It outlines a fundamental *experience of the world* on an empirical level. It always evokes it anew with the typical immediacy of sense perception. In order to explain this experience, let us ask what natural being is when it is manifested as raw being. What matters now is no longer the mode and occasion of such a manifestation, but its content. What is nature insofar as it always preserves an uncertain outline? What is the sensible that really shows itself only if it remains unfocused?

Visible being is raw if it does not contract into the discrete unities, independent from one another, which we designate as 'objects'. The absence of form makes nature present itself as a compact *continuum*, a manifold that is not subject to a synthesis, and an enveloping matter. (We could say that objects are broken down into an indivisible *continuum* when visual representation imitates the perceptive modalities of the senses that are heterogeneous from it, thus trying to account for what pertains exclusively to the sense of touch, hearing, taste and smell.) Sensible being is raw if it is eternally contiguous, conterminous, and *adjacent*; it influences in a decisive manner what happens at centre stage but has no role in the play. The sensible is raw if it *bends itself*, spreading to the side of and behind the one who looks. The sensible is raw if (unlike an object) it never lies *in front*, but always and only *all around*. In conclusion, the sensible is raw as a pure and simple *context*; or better, as *the* context in which every entity is located, all facts happen, and any discourse resonates.

While the ocean, the desert, or other particular phenomena are here out of the question, what is at stake is also no longer simply the mere effects of looking out of the corner of one's eye. Matter as a whole is always already amorphous as the *context* of our existence. Conversely, matter delineates a context—a *world*—precisely because it is also amorphous; if matter were articulated and specified in each of its aspects, it would give rise only to a 'vital sphere'—an *environment* (in which the animal is stuck in an univocal and definitive way). One is *situated* in the formless context, whereas one is *included* in the hyper-structured environment; one belongs to the former, however, without fully adhering to it (since we are indeed dealing with a generic and undetermined matter); one is bound to the latter down to the last detail, as if it were a functional prosthesis. Experiencing 'raw nature' therefore means experiencing the world. Through the perception of the contextual sensible we certainly do not get to know *how* the world is, but we acknowledge with wonder *that* it is.

The material context, just like the 'totality of nature' of which Kant speaks, eludes every representation. There is no adequate imagination for a *continuum* devoid of punctuations, a manifold resistant to synthesis, and a perennially unfocused sensible. There is no assertion capable of reflecting what does not stand *in front of* but *all around* us. Since it remains unreachable for the faculty of representation, amorphous matter deserves the name of *non-empirical sensible*. However, the iconoclastic inclination of the *context* has nothing in common with that of *totality*; the apparent analogy actually disguises a radical antithesis.

While the 'totality of nature' is irrepresentable because it can only be *thought*, the material context is instead irrepresentable because it can only be *perceived*. In the first case, we obtain concepts freed from sensation; in the second, sensations without a concept.

Moreover, the irrepresentable *thought* of nature as a totality liquidates its own object—nature—evoking instead a 'supersensible destination'; on the contrary, insofar as the *perception* of the context itself exceeds representation, it is a witness to a sensible being that transcends the synthetic functions of the 'I think'. 'Raw nature' is felt by means of countless *infinitesimal small perceptions*[11] that surpass self-consciousness, circumscribing its field of action and limiting its power. We perceive much more than we know we perceive—and hence much more than we are able to represent. But it is precisely this *perceptual surplus* that locates the perceiver in an overwhelming material context, preliminarily correlating him 'with all the rest of the universe'.[12] The state of mind Kant calls mathematical sublime in fact originates from the unbridgeable discrepancy between the raw sensible and formed nature, the look out of the corner of one's eye and perspectival vision, the contextual *continuum* and discrete unities, small perceptions and self-consciousness.

On the one hand, amorphous nature, which functions as a context for every experience and representation, never fails (like a horizon). On the other, however, it always remains *unrealized*, as a possibility whose accomplishment is definitively precluded. It is unfailing but only *potential*; this is the salient characteristic of the raw (or non-empirical) sensible, the one that condenses and clarifies all those we have examined so far. This adjacent and unfocused sensible materially subsists but in the way of a pure *dynamis* or *non-actualizable potency*. A well-formed entity, characterized by certain essential properties, is 'possible' if it still does not exist (to put it as Kant does: if a sensation is not added to its concept); when it comes to existence, it becomes a 'real' entity—an entity whose essential properties have been realized. Vice versa, the lack of form—which ultimately

---

11 See Gottfried Wilhelm Leibniz, *New Essays Concerning Human Understanding* (London: Macmillan, 1896), pp. 48ff.

12 Leibniz, *New Essays*, p. 48.

amounts to the lack of any essential property—implies instead an existence split from realization, that is, a merely potential existence. Generic or formless matter, which constitutes the field in which every well-formed entity is inscribed, always already exists, without, for this reason, abandoning the status of the 'possible', and without rising to the rank of the 'real'. With regard to raw nature, we should say that it is eternally possible, because it elicits sensations to which a concept is never added.

Paraphrasing Merleau-Ponty,[13] who speaks of a 'flesh of the world', it seems appropriate to refer to the contextual sensible as the *flesh of the possible*. 'Flesh', since this possible is nevertheless a visible and tangible matter; it puts pressure on the edges of the gaze. It looms closely, bends itself all around, and is exhibited by the perceptions that surpass representation. 'Of the possible', since the existence of this matter does not entail—or better excludes—a realization, and rather proves its worth as an absolute *dynamis* or inextinguishable virtuality.

Unrealizability is therefore a constitutive trait of the world. When the metaphysical tradition conceives of the world-context as an unattainable *totality* of the finite intellect, it misunderstands this unrealizability up to the point of reversing its meaning. In fact, the material context is unrealizable as a consequence of its permanent potentiality, and certainly not because of a limit of knowledge; instead, totality surpasses human knowledge precisely because it amounts to the *total realization* of every potentiality. The expressions 'unattainable totality' and 'unrealizable context', which seem to be combined at first sight, are actually antinomic and incompatible. Metaphysical cosmology makes us think of a world that is brought into focus in all its aspects—as actualized, complete, concluded. Kant writes that reason 'requires totality [. . .] and does not exempt

---

13 Maurice Merleau-Ponty, *The Visible and the Invisible* (Evanston, IL: Northwestern University Press, 1969).

from this requirement even the infinite [. . .], but rather makes it unavoidable for us to think it as *given entirely* (in its totality)'.[14] The world as a 'limited whole' of which Wittgenstein speaks in the *Tractatus* is itself given entirely, that is, redeemed from every remaiing contingency.

As soon as we try to realize (as a totality) the lasting potentiality of the world-context, we fall into infinite regression. In other words, cosmological regression originates at the moment when we confuse what is only *possible* with something *incomplete*. The attempt to give form to 'raw nature' has no outcome, or better, results in the 'bad infinity' denounced by Hegel. Intending to fully determine the contextual 'all around', as if it were an articulated 'in front', we always again, and in vain, go back to the 'ascending regressive series' of cosmological conditions. At each step, with *tedious* repetitiveness, the very limit we seemed to have overcome re-emerges. We can discern an indirect proof of the unrealizability of the world-context (or of the persistent potentiality of the sensible as amorphous) in the very fact that regression cannot be concluded. However, for Kant and Wittgenstein, this inconcludability—which is ascribed to the insufficiency of the human intellect—only indicates that totality is a *transcendent* idea. The accomplishment of the regressive series is guaranteed by a supersensible 'unconditioned condition', whose recognition would require us to go beyond the transient world. In this way, the 'unattainability of nature' as *raw* nature is turned into the overcoming of nature in general.

The metaphysical idea of the world as totality postulates the surreptitious realization of what is exclusively possible. Once again, for this reason, it generates the interminable cosmological regression, on the one hand, and 'concludes' it by resorting to an extramundane and all in all transcendent principle, on the other. We now need to ask whether there nevertheless exists an adequate idea, measure, or

---

14 Kant, *Critique of the Power of Judgment*, p. 138 (emphasis added).

expression for the world as material context, that is, for the *flesh of the possible*. What is finally the idea, *eidos*, or appearance of the sensible as only potential? To answer this, it is useful to hint at the *fundamental experience of language*, which is always again betrayed (that is, exhibited and distorted at the same time) by infinite meta-linguistic regression.

3.3 FATHER AND SON

Let us recall what Wittgenstein writes in the *Lecture on Ethics*: 'I am tempted to say that the right expression in language for the miracle of the existence of the world, though it is not any proposition *in* language, is the existence of language itself.'[15] The event of Creation (the existence of the world) is redoubled into the event of the Word (the existence of language); the latter prolongs and mirrors the former. According to Wittgenstein, the relation that is in force between the fact that there is the world and the fact that there is language is the same as the one that unites Father and Son in the New Testament: 'God the Father created the world, while God the Son (or the Word proceeding from God) is the ethical.'[16] Accounting discursively for the existence of language, that is, for what enables every discourse, would also mean expressing the world as a 'limited whole'; a truly successful self-reference would unravel at the same time the cosmological question. But, for Wittgenstein, there is no statement that is able to represent the very fact that we speak; just as the Father 'does not reveal himself *in* the world' he created, so the Son—the Word—does not reveal himself *in* language. The deadlock to which linguistic self-reference is doomed amounts to the New Testament version of Kant's mathematical sublime; in fact, it is precisely the inevitable failure that indicates always anew, by hitting the limit, the divine nature of the Word (that is, the Son).

---

15 Wittgenstein, *Lecture on Ethics*, p. 52.

16 Wittgenstein, *Wittgenstein and the Vienna*, p. 118.

At the end of the *Lecture*, Wittgenstein admits that, by speaking about the good and the meaning of life, he intended '*to go beyond the world* and *that is to say* beyond significant language'.[17] The limit is one and the same; the overcoming would also be one and the same. But is the 'that is to say' so obvious? What is the belief that the transcendence of the world certainly coincides with that of language based on? We are authorized, and even obliged, to postulate such a coincidence only if we presuppose a strong connection between names and objects, assertions and facts, signifying expressions and mundane state of affairs. In order to have the same edges and a common limit, language and the world must be *coextensive* and biunivocally correspond to each other point by point. The *denotative* relation between words and things, as the apparent emblem of 'this side' ['*al di qua*'], envisions an identical (and evidently unreachable) 'other side' ['*al di là*'].

The manifest complicity between denotation and transcendence solicits, by contrast, a series of radical questions. What are the consequences of the abandonment of the presupposition of coextensiveness, that is, the critique of the correspondence between assertions and facts? Insofar as the limit of the world no longer corresponds with that of language, the overcoming of the former is *not* also the overcoming of the latter. Furthermore, if differentiated and bifurcated, is transcendence still transcendent? Was the 'that is to say' only a determination added to transcendence or did it constitute its ground? When we consider the 'beyond' ['*al di là*'] of the world as *distinct* from the 'beyond' of language, are we still dealing, in both cases, with an actual 'beyond'? As soon as the denotative symbiosis is dissolved, language and the world show their full asymmetry and heterogeneity; rather than mirroring one another like parallel straight lines, they intersect, reciprocally limit each other, and still reciprocally overcome each other. But, then, should we not think that the 'beyond' of the world falls *within* language (thus ceasing to be a

---

17 Wittgenstein, *Lecture on Ethics*, p. 53 (second emphasis added).

'beyond')? What if the existence of the world is *signified* by certain inconspicuous ways of saying? And, conversely, should we not think that the 'beyond' of language falls *within* the world (thus ceasing to be a 'beyond')? What if the existence of language is *situated* in an overpowering sensible context?

These—obviously rhetorical—questions are nothing but a road sign; they indicate an argumentative direction, which I can here cover only rapidly.

3.4 THE INSERTION OF LANGUAGE

When we ascertain with wonder that language exists, we do not refer to the set of all possible propositions, but to the possibility of enunciating any proposition. Language is a *faculty*; it exists as a potency that is never fully realized. We can recognize a structural analogy between language [*lingua*] and the raw sensible: like the context perceived out of the corner of one's eye, having-speech [*l'aver-parola*] is itself an inexhaustible virtuality, which knows no accomplishment, or better, is perfectly accomplished precisely insofar as it remains non-actualizable or 'amorphous'. Language, which does not *stand for* the world (nor mirror or correspond to it), nonetheless shares with the world the way of being of an inextinguishable *dynamis*. The infinite regression of the metalanguages (whose *sublime* failure seems to hint at the transcendent nature of the Word-Son) in fact emerges from the attempt to represent the faculty of speech as a *fully given totality*. Not unlike cosmological regression, it aspires to complete, that is, realize, what is instead only possible.

Moreover, the faculty of speech—the mere power-of-saying [*poter-dire*]—is not a guaranteed possession; so much so that, in infancy, we cannot *yet* speak, and, in the event of aphasic disturbances, we can no *longer* speak. If the child is an aphasic person on the road to recovery, the aphasic person is a chronic child. Both are cross-border workers; the former migrates into language, while the latter is evicted from it like a tenant in arrears. They meet at the border, where access and exit coincide. The existence of language as a faculty, always missed by the reverse gear of the 'discourse on discourse', is exhibited instead by the linguistic phenomena connected with the *doing* and *undoing* of speech (to quote the Italian title of a well-known book by Roman Jakobson devoted to the symmetry between child language and aphasia[18]). However, this exhibition of the very fact that we speak (as an early and insecure 'fact', itself afflicted by contingency) would not be possible if a forced silence or an empirical deficiency were at stake. But the experience of the child and the sick person—for whom language is a virtuality or latency—is not located at the periphery of verbal behaviour, as a mere negative determination and a chronological or pathological interlude. On the contrary, this experience of language as something that *may* be, which can be accessed or removed, pervades discourse as undamaged and well formed, and is always again confirmed by some of its all-round performances.

There are efficient functions and structures of language that introject the poverty of the aphasic, and regular ways of saying that extract their logical form from an impasse of communication. The incompleteness and virtuality of language are shown by phrases that do not lack anything; the 'not yet' and 'no longer' of the power-of-saying find a positive articulation in full and ductile statements. Now, we need to recognize the place of a radical *self-reflection* of human speech in the regions of normal discourse that contain the aphasic experience—and offer its other side. It is in fact precisely there that language accounts for itself as an *event*, since it shows that it *is* (insofar as the phrase takes place without problems), while it may *not be* (insofar as the phrase adopts the peculiar traits of a kind of *inability-to-say*

---

18 Roman Jakobson, *Il farsi e il disfarsi del linguaggio: Linguaggio infantile e afasia* [The Doing and Undoing of Language. Child Language and Aphasia] (Turin: Einaudi, 1971).

[*non-poter-dire*]). This is a kind of self-reflection that goes against the metaphysical idea of language as always *presupposed* to itself; it is therefore completely alien to the interminable backwards flight of metalanguages. We are rather dealing with ordinary ways of saying that, having an 'aphasic' root, attest *with words* to the limits and instability of speech—they *eloquently* evoke the possibility that speech [*eloquio*] may not be.

The logical framework of the *modality of the possible* thoroughly corresponds point by point to the identifying marks of one of the main types of aphasia. The usual propositional formulas with which we form a hypothetical discourse ('it is possible that . . . ', etc.) amount to the highlighted counterpart, in itself perfectly accomplished, of a specific limitation of communicative skills. Elsewhere I explained this isomorphism in great detail and attempted to demonstrate it;[19] here I can only outline it in an apodictic way.

In his 'Reference and Modality',[20] Willard V.O. Quine defines the statements pertaining to the realm of the possible as 'opaque contexts', since in them the correspondence between words and things (on which the transparency of discourse depends) seems to be fading away—as if it were indefinitely suspended by a sort of magnetic storm. According to Quine, the crisis of denotation—the opacity of the context—is proved by the fact that the grammatical subject of a modal statement cannot be replaced without complications by an identical term. Let us clarify this with an example. Once we have agreed upon the identity of two linguistic signs, such as 'Tegucigalpa' = 'capital of Honduras', in order to establish whether in a given assertion the name 'Tegucigalpa' is used in a denotative way (that is, whether it *stands for* something), it is enough to replace it with the

---

19 Paolo Virno, *Parole con parole: Poteri e limiti del linguaggio* (Rome: Donzelli, 1995), pp. 133–42.

20 Willard V.O. Quine, 'Reference and Modality' in *From a Logical Point of View* (Cambridge, MA: Harvard University Press, 1961), pp. 139–57.

equivalent 'capital of Honduras'; if the translation does not alter the meaning of the assertion, then 'Tegucigalpa' definitely has a referential value. But such a translation is precisely interdicted by an 'opaque context'. If in the modal statement 'it is possible that Tegucigalpa will no longer be the capital of Honduras,' I replace 'Tegucigalpa' with its synonym, I obtain a blatant absurdity: 'It is possible that the capital of Honduras will no longer be the capital of Honduras.'

The indisposition to replace demonstrates that, when the possible is at stake, the grammatical subject does not have any denotative role, since its meaning is strictly bound to the *context*. In addition to blocking the 'biunivocal relation between names and reality', at the same time and for the same reasons, the pre-eminence of the context also dismisses the employment of metalanguage. In order to establish the identity between two names ('Tegucigalpa' and 'capital of Honduras'), which enables us to express the correspondence between name and object, it is necessary to speak of one's code, that is, carry out a discourse *about* discourse. It goes without saying that this metalinguistic move is precluded where the opacity of the context prevents us from the outset to equate the grammatical subject with any other term. Denotation, identity, and metalanguage are concepts that support one another: they stand or fall together. The modality of the possible abrogates the whole lot.

Although it is evocative, the expression 'opaque context' is nonetheless pleonastic; in fact, should there be no opacity, neither will there be a context. When the latter holds its ground, the correspondence between words and things is *always* opaque. The hypothesis of a 'transparent context' (as proposed by Quine), in which the referentiality of the name and the meta-linguistic operations have free rein, is only a discrete way of alluding to the conceptual abolition of the very notion of 'context'. Avoiding the pleonasm, it is therefore legitimate to state (against Quine) that, far from amounting to an occasional perturbation, the modality of the possible lets us grasp the contextual nature of language in general—the being-in-context of every speaker. Or better, the modality of the possible shows *the insertion of language into the world*.

Let us now consider the connection between the discourse on the possible and a given aphasic deficiency. Roman Jakobson distinguishes two fundamental kinds of aphasia. In the first, what is impaired is the ability to *select* within the linguistic code the terms that need to be employed, while the inclination to *combine* given elements of that same code remains undamaged; the individual is able to continue sentences that have already begun, but not to start new ones. In the second kind, the selective function is instead preserved, while the combinatory one is in ruin; the individual is limited to the *incipit* of sentences that can however not be developed. Now, the statements characterized by the presence of the possible are the non-pathological counterpart of the first kind of aphasia.

When the faculty of selection is damaged, the connective texture of the proposition survives, but the terms endowed with a marked autonomy fall apart. Jakobson writes that 'the most viable elements are those which serve to construct sentences, the so-called little words, such as connectives, pronouns, etc. [. . .] The initial substantive of the sentence presents the greatest difficulty.'[21] The *primacy of the context* goes together with the *crisis of the* grammatical *subject*. The aphasic safely and skilfully wanders in a given discursive field, yet sinks into quicksand when he approaches its border. The contextual bound, which is reinforced by the impediment of selection, involves the absolute impossibility of *replacing* an isolated term with another of identical value, as well as the factual atrophy of metalanguage. Jakobson observes that a normal speaker is also able to 'talk about language itself'; if he believes he may be misunderstood when he uses the word 'champagne', he will promptly replace it with the word

---

21 Roman Jakobson, 'Linguistic Types of Aphasia' in *Selected Writings: Volume 2, Word and Language* (The Hague: Mouton, 1971), p. 311.

'French sparkling white wine', and thus speak about the very code through which he expresses himself. This move is precisely what is inhibited in the aphasic: 'The use of language to discuss language, labelled "metalanguage" in logic, is deficient in aphasics with a selection disorder.'[22]

The inconveniences and oddities Quine attributes to the modality of the possible are also the symptoms of the pathology studied by Jakobson. Just as we are not *logically* allowed to replace 'Tegucigalpa' with the equivalent 'capital of Honduras' in the opaque context 'it is possible that Tegucigalpa will no longer be the capital of Honduras', so too the translation of 'champagne' as 'French sparkling white wine' is *materially* precluded for the aphasic. The criterion of replaceability, advocated by Quine to ascertain the denotative use of the name, is a minefield for the sick person. He quickly loses both the meaning and the reference of the individual substantive; in fact, as soon as the intra-linguistic commutation between 'champagne' and 'French sparkling white wine' is obstructed, the semantic content of both terms fades away and their ability to stand for a given object vanishes. The aphasia in question paralyzes at the same time the denotative and meta-linguistic functions, and thus negatively demonstrates their collusion: 'The aphasic defect in the "capacity of naming" is properly a loss of metalanguage.'[23]

There is only one, yet decisive, difference between the pathological flaw of the selective function and the statements on the possible. The *same* indigence that is signalled by the interruption of discourse in the former results from a perfectly accomplished discourse in the latter—it inheres to the full presence of speech. In the modality of

---

22 Roman Jakobson, 'Aphasia as a Linguistic Topic' in *Selected Writings: Volume 2, Word and Language*, p. 235.

23 Roman Jakobson, 'Two Aspects of Language and Two Types of Aphasic Disturbances' in *Selected Writings: Volume 2, Word and Language*, p. 248.

the possible, the limitation is not unfolded as a blight of names, but is inoculated in the logical form of enunciation. Instead of being limited to the unattainability of certain elements of the linguistic code, here the 'aphasic' defect concerns the position of the whole code with respect to the field of vital experience. It is no longer the connective texture of the sentence but the field that now delineates the unavoidable sphere the speaker relies on without owning its *incipit*— that is, with an exclusively 'combinatory' predisposition. For those who say 'it is possible that . . . ', the unavoidable *context* that prevails over the subject is the *sensible world* to which we belong. Instead of denoting the sensible world as something that lies 'in front' of us, the modal statements inscribe themselves in it in the guise of 'little words', which articulate and connect but do not start a sentence.

Once it is transposed into the modality of the possible, that is, of regular discourse, the aphasic experience described by Jakobson as 'a flight from identity towards contiguity' thereby concerns the very relation between language and the world. This relation amounts to an incomplete interpretation and an always imperfect deciphering. The modal functor 'it is possible that' shows the hermeneutic limit of human speech with respect to the sensible context in which it resonates; in other words, it shows how, not being fully able to cope with this context, enunciation locates itself in an extra-linguistic sphere that overwhelms it and remains opaque to it.

However, to state that the modality of the possible exposes the relation between language and the world—as a relation characterized by an insufficient deciphering—could give rise to misunderstandings. The risk here is corroborating the vulgar image of a world that is presupposed to (and independent from) language, which then happens to be partly resistant to being represented by means of names and assertions. Obviously, this is not the case. On the contrary, it is precisely the hermeneutic weakness of language that turns the world into a 'world'. It is only when speech shows its deficient decoding with regard to the non-linguistic sphere that the latter presents itself as an unsurpassable context, and thus configures itself as a *world*. Verging on a paradox, we could also say that *the world is linguistically constituted by what, in language, manifests the incompleteness or limitation of language with respect to the world*. Ultimately, the fact that humankind has a 'world' (with regard to which interpenetration is always imperfect, conflict unsolved, and orientation partial and precarious) rather than an 'environment' (into which one is instead irrevocably integrated as in an amniotic fluid) is due to the *limits of language*, not to its representational power.

3.5 CHIASM

Let us sum this up. The existence of the world as a *context*—unattainable because of the cosmological infinite regression, whose aim is to realize the context as a fully given *totality*—is experienced in the phenomenon of sensible or 'raw' nature, which is only adjacent and always potential. The existence of language as a *faculty*—never touched by the meta-linguistic infinite regression, which is rather focused on realizing the faculty as a fully actual *totality*—is experienced in well-formed clauses that, adopting the logical structure of aphasia, highlight the power-of-saying against the background of its limitations, bottlenecks, and eclipses. The most important among those regular clauses that have an 'aphasic' matrix is the modality of the possible. In fact, the modality of the possible accounts for the relation language has with the material world; this is at the same time a deficient and decisive relation (or better, decisive precisely insofar as it is deficient) from which every kind of coextension and 'correspondence' is excluded. The intersection between *context* and *faculty* constitutes the real centre of gravity of the state of mind Kant calls mathematical sublime and Wittgenstein miraculous wonder. This intersection has the shape of a chiasm; context and faculty cross like the abscissa and the ordinate; or better, each term is the *beyond*, the *measure*, and the *unconditioned condition* of the other.

First of all, the modality of the possible exhibits the inscription of language *in* the world—it shows how the very power-of-saying is included in an exorbitant sensible context. In this sense, the world circumscribes and overwhelms speech; it is its *beyond*. However, on the other hand, the contextual character of raw nature is brought to light only thanks to the insertion—in raw nature—of articulated discourse; finite or 'aphasic' speech institutes always again the sphere that exceeds speech. In this sense, language gives rise to the world; it is its *beyond*. Far from implying one and the same transcendence (which would have as a content the unity of the Father-Creator with the Son-Speech), language and the world, faculty and context, power-of-saying and formless sensible, transcend one another, or, in other words, limit one another. However, the *mundane* 'beyond' of language is not an authentic 'beyond', but rather something that can still be *perceived*. Likewise, the *linguistic* 'beyond' of the world is not an authentic 'beyond', but rather something that can still be *uttered*.

Secondly, the way of being of both the context and the faculty is an unrealisable *dynamis*, or a persistent virtuality. However, precisely for this reason, neither the context nor the faculty benefit from a defined aspect, an autonomous appearance, or an expression appropriate to them. What is only potential—the amorphous sensible or the power-of-saying—does not have in itself its own *eidos*, measure, and physiognomy. This point is outlined by Kant when he claims that the deadlock of the imagination in assessing 'the immeasurability of nature' evokes 'another, nonsensible measure';[24] but also by Wittgenstein, for whom the collision against the limits of language reveals, so to speak, a *non-linguistic measure* of our faculty of speech. However, for Kant, the 'unalterable [non-sensible] basic measure of nature is its absolute *totality*.'[25] And, coinciding with a total

---

24 Kant, *Critique of the Power of Judgment*, p. 145.
25 Kant, *Critique of the Power of Judgment*, p. 139 (emphasis added).

realization, totality distorts and cancels the eternally potential character of the world-context and of the language-faculty. How, then,
do things really stand? It is certainly the case that a non-actualisable
dynamis finds its own measure (or idea) only outside itself—in something *heterogeneous*; but, although it is of a different kind, this something cannot but be, in turn, a pure *dynamis*. The inexhaustible
potentiality of the raw sensible provides the faculty of language with
a physiognomy, an *eidos*, and a 'non-linguistic measure'. Reciprocally,
the power-of-saying constitutes the heterogeneous appearance, the
eidos, and the 'non-sensible measure' of amorphous and unfocused
nature, that is to say, of what we earlier called the *flesh of the possible*.
Devoid of an image that is its own, the unrealisable context offers an
appearance to the unrealisable faculty; and the latter offers it an
oblique semblance.

Thirdly, the intersection between language and the world concludes, or better interrupts, both cosmological and meta-linguistic
regression. It is their common outcome. Moreover, this intersection
is the point where the linear backward march reveals its original cur-
vature, that is, refutes itself showing that it is not really a regression
but, indeed, a circular movement.

The monotonous spiral of the discourse-on-discourse is arrested
as soon as it issues into the non-linguistic side of the intersection
between language and the world; its 'unconditioned condition' is the
sensible context, which also delimits and locates the power-of-saying.
This condition turns out to be actually 'unconditioned' (that is, determining but undeterminable) because it is *heterogeneous* to the series
that depends on it. Meta-linguistic regression is completed by the perception of raw nature; it thus ends with a *metabasis eis allo genos*—a
passage into another kind of experience. After all, we saw how it is
precisely and only raw nature that gives us the 'measure' of language
(that measure or *eidos* that the discourse-on-discourse instead pursues
in vain). In a fully analogous way, cosmological regression is
exhausted and stops when it approaches its own heterogeneous

'unconditioned condition', namely, the faculty of speech that, while inscribing itself into the world-context, also establishes the world-context. Even in this case, we have a passage into another kind—the infinitesimal small perceptions—which elude representation and hint at the merely contextual sensible, finding an indirect accomplishment, or an oblique integration, in the experience of the power-of-saying. After all, as we also saw, it is precisely and only the inconsumable *dynamis* of language that provides a 'measure'—an *eidos*—for raw nature.

3.6 'SUCH INDOLENT MODESTY'

What is the state of mind correlated with the *interruption* of cosmological and meta-linguistic regression that we deemed to be infinite? What emotional aspect accompanies (or rather reveals) the chiasm between the faculty of language and the amorphous sensible? In short, what is the *feeling of the context*? If infinite regression causes boredom, and, according to Leopardi, boredom is 'the desire for happiness left pure', we then need to assume that, once regression has stopped, this pure desire can appear in a guise that is completely different from boredom.

We know that the interminable backwards flight of the meta-languages and cosmological points of view is stimulated by the presumption of being able to grasp as an actual totality what instead exists only in the modality of the possible. This presumption contaminates the idea of happiness, which is conceived as a complete passage from potency to the act, and thus as an absolute 'realization' of ourselves in the world and of the world in ourselves. However, given that the non-actualizable *dynamis* always postpones its effective accomplishment, the aspiration for happiness fatally turns into the 'vivid sense of the nothingness of all things'—tedium. Instead, following Aristotle's definition of happiness, how is the search for the 'good that is always desirable in itself and never for the sake of something else'[26] manifested once we acknowledge the constitutively unrealizable character of the world (and of us in it)? Evidently, what is at stake is no longer a progressive draining of the *dynamis*, but the inclination to inhabit the very 'flesh of the possible'. This inclination consists of making the eternal potentiality of the world-context resonate in every single event and object. The accomplished fact or the well-determined thing let the profile of something raw and amorphous—a contextual nuance—transpire; among their essential properties we should also include the power-of-being-otherwise, a lasting suspension between antithetical developments, and unsettled contingency. The experience of the world withdrawn from infinite regression is characterized by the integral preservation of the set of possibilities enclosed by a particular *hic et nunc*. If it is embedded in such an experience, the desire for happiness promptly maintains itself beside *facts* and *things* (it rather is their 'vivid sense'), since every fact and thing can exhibit in itself, through a sort of trite miracle, the *dynamis* of the context to which it belongs. In Walter Benjamin's words, the instance of happiness finds an adequate foothold in the Newhaven fishwife, photographed in the early twentieth century with 'her eyes cast down in such indolent, seductive modesty', because 'in the immediacy of that long-forgotten moment the future'—that is, the possible—'nests so eloquently'.[27]

These are only a few evocative hints. In order to fully grasp the state of mind that arises from the interruption of infinite regression and characterizes the experience of the world-context, it is necessary to critically discuss the other form of sublime analysed by Kant—the dynamical sublime, that is to say, the feeling of absolute safety. For Kant, the 'unconditioned condition' of nature, which the

---

26 Aristotle, *Nichomachean Ethics* 1097a 30–34.

27 Walter Benjamin, 'Little History of Photography' in *Selected Writings: Volume 2, Part 2, 1931–34* (Cambridge, MA: Harvard University Press, 1999), p. 510.

mathematical sublime exhibits negatively, is also what, from an ethical standpoint, guarantees protection and meaning to our existence. The drive to *totality* is merged with the search for an unassailable *shelter*. We now need to ask on what conditions the *feeling of the context* (as the materialist counterpart of the mathematical sublime) can generate comfort and safety. What is its 'dynamical', or better ethical, implication? Our distance from the Kantian scheme is clear. Totality offers a solid shelter because it overcomes and dismisses the sensible world as the source of every danger. On the contrary, the material context protects us in virtue of the same quality that renders it threatening, namely, its unrealizable potentiality. The very same kernel of experience may turn out to be uncanny or comforting, frightening or redeeming. As we will see, the conversion of the *dynamis* from imminent danger into reassuring abode takes place when the perception of the sensible context—raw nature—is redoubled as the establishment of a different 'all around': the *public sphere*.

4.
Public Sphere

4.1 THE NAMELESS THREAT

The dynamical sublime takes as its starting point the feeling of relief that pervades us when we enjoy being sheltered against the raging of one or another calamity (be it a smallpox epidemic, an earthquake, or the attentions of the Ministry of Interior). Averting a given danger sharpens the awareness of our defencelessness but also makes us superior to chance and fate. Albeit in itself temporary and extremely fragile, such a superiority gives rise to the thought of its lasting equivalent, namely, the independence of the moral Self from nature and the course of the world. The fortuitous protection from a specific disaster evokes the possibility of a shelter that is instead *absolute* —'our power (which is not part of nature) to regard those things about which we are concerned (goods, health and life) as trivial, and hence to regard natural power (to which we are, to be sure, subjected in regard to these things) as not the sort of dominion over ourselves and our person'.[1] Finally, the dynamical sublime is the empirical foreboding of that unconditioned immunity which only compliance with

---

[1] Kant, *Critique of the Power of Judgment*, p. 145.

the moral law can provide us. According to Wittgenstein, the miraculous discovery of a free zone exempted from any risk 'has been described by saying that we feel safe in the hands of God'.[2]

But what does the danger that requires, as its sole antidote, 'the experience of feeling absolutely safe' consist of? And, above all, how is it announced? In the short treatise *Of the Sublime* (1793), written shortly after *Critique of the Power of Judgment* and under its clear influence, Schiller observes that the dynamical sublime 'is grounded in no way whatsoever in the conquest or cancellation of a danger threatening us, but rather upon the clearing away of the last condition, under which alone there can be danger for us'.[3] Now, the 'last condition' of risk is our very belonging to the world, or, as Schiller adds, 'the sensuous part of our being'. The world is absolute jeopardy, undetermined and omnilateral dangerousness, threatening pressure that heralds every particular threat and makes it possible. Its non-actualizable *dynamis*, to which we are constantly exposed, unleashes a shapeless destructive force. Heidegger defines *anxiety* as the shapeless fear—not ascribable to a specific cause and yet impending—instilled by the overpowering context in which our existence takes place: 'That about which one has anxiety is being-in-the-world as such.'[4] Insofar as it expresses a drive to unconditioned safety, *the feeling of the dynamical sublime is always related to anxiety*—the emotional situation of total vulnerability in which the world is manifested as the 'last condition' of danger.

Ailment and cure correspond with one another following a perfect symmetry. For Kant, there is an extreme difference between the

---

2 Ludwig Wittgenstein, 'A Lecture on Ethics', *The Philosophical Review* 74 (1) (1965): 3–12; here, p. 10.

3 Friedrich Schiller, *Of the Sublime* (William F. Wertz trans.) (Washington: Schiller Institute, 2001) (available at: https://bit.ly/3987O0i; last accessed 1 June 2022).

4 Martin Heidegger, *Being and Time* (Albany: SUNY Press, 2010), p. 180.

occasional physical shelter, which safeguards us from a flood or a conspiracy, and the absolute protection from the vehemence of the
world, which is instead guaranteed to us by the moral law. For
Heidegger, a similarly unbridgeable gap separates fear from anxiety.
What frightens us is a given event, a circumscribed state of affairs, a
defined object. Fright can be alleviated by appropriate factual expe-
dients; an *ad hoc* shelter pertinent to the circumstances is enough. On
the contrary, anxiety is not bound to one or another state of affairs;
it does not arise on predictable occasions; it laughs at every wise
attempt to inhibit or mitigate it. When we fall prey to anxiety, 'the
world has the character of complete insignificance.'⁵ The threat is
equally pressing and generic; danger has no face or name; it is everywhere and nowhere: 'What anxiety is about is completely indefinite.'⁶
The dynamical sublime is the state of mind elicited by the disproportion between fear and anxiety; or better, by the discrepancy between
what manages to restrain fear and that absolute safety which alone
could save us from anxiety.

Previously we saw how, being embedded in infinite regression,
the mathematical sublime is intimately connected with the experience
of tedium. We have now ascertained the strict affinity between the
dynamical sublime and anxiety. Those who wish to look for a thematic
equivalent of the Kantian 'Analytic of the Sublime' in Heidegger's
work need to pay attention to the investigation of boredom carried
out in his 1929–1930 lectures (and subsequently published as *The Fundamental Concepts of Metaphysics*) and to paragraph 40 of *Being and
Time*, in which he illustrates the mood of anxiety. According to
Heidegger, when we are steeped in profound boredom—of the kind
that does not depend on a setback and cannot be chased away
through some expedient—'we find ourselves in the midst of beings
as a whole'; or rather, in the midst of 'beings' refusal of themselves

---

5 Heidegger, *Being and Time*, p. 180.
6 Heidegger, *Being and Time*, p. 180.

as a whole', that is, at 'the point where all and everything appears indifferent to us'.[7] This negative whole is the world—but, so to speak, the world in its 'entire magnitude', that is, understood mathematically. On the other hand, anxiety, which 'takes one's breath away'[8] and imposes 'the existential "mode" of *not-being-at-home*',[9] reveals the world in its threatening power, as understood dynamically. However, here we are not really interested in the play of mirrors between two philosophers. As was the case with regard to infinite regression and tedium, we have to critically consider the concepts of 'anxiety' and 'absolute safety'. What matters is figuring out in a different way the mode of being to which they refer; or, if you wish, elaborating differently the idea of world as a fearsome contingency.

4.2 DREAD AND SHELTER

In the first place, we need to call into question the distinction between fear and anxiety as well as the corresponding division between factual safety and absolute shelter. Both these polar couples are based on the persistence, or at least the vivid memory, of traditional communities in which a network of consolidated habits channels praxis, protecting it from randomness. The divergence of fear and anxiety follows from the fracture that opposes a familiar environment, within which experience is cyclical, uniform, and well-articulated, to the vast and undetermined world. The dangers filtered and alleviated by the communitarian *ethos* cause only fear; we can come to terms with them, expect and contain them, and at times even avoid them. Anxiety is instead triggered when we venture—mentally or factually—beyond this border into the amorphous world-context. Threats become continuous and ubiquitous there, without us being able to

---

7 Martin Heidegger, *The Fundamental Concept of Metaphysics: World, Finitude, Solitude* (Bloomington: Indiana University Press, 1995), pp. 137–8.

8 Heidegger, *Being and Time*, p. 180.

9 Heidegger, *Being and Time*, p. 183.

decipher their nature and isolate their cause. But the hiatus between the two forms of dread (and of safety) fades away after the collapse of the last substantial communities; it is sutured at the end of every social or ethical arrangement that boasts the almost immutable stability of an 'environment', and thereby proves to be 'poor-in-world' (using the expression with which Heidegger qualifies the *habitat* of animals).

The permanent variability of the forms of life, the uninterrupted undoing of habits that are already in themselves artificial and contingent, and the training aimed at facing a limitless randomness all involve a direct relationship with the *raw* world—an immediate confrontation with the 'last condition' of danger. Fear is always *anguished*, since the pervasive and undetermined threatening character of the world-context explicitly converges on the particular cause that triggers it. Reciprocally, anxiety is always *fearful*—it acquires an empirical-factual aspect. Anxiety hinges on objects and states of affairs, because they in turn present a high degree of uncertainty and unsolved potentiality (and thus fall into line with the typical traits of the world-context). We therefore need to introduce a concept that accounts for the irreversible combination of the two emotional situations that were previously separated. I will return to this point.

My second critical consideration is actually a corollary to what we have just said. The gap between fear and anxiety entails a disconcerting outcome; while the former would be a feeling that can be communicated, shared, and somehow *public*, the latter would instead favour the most radical isolation. For Heidegger, 'anxiety individualizes and thus discloses Dasein as *"solus ipse"'*; in it, the 'Dasein-with of others [. . .] can offer nothing more'.[10] Unlike fear, fuelled by a danger that often concerns many members of the community and can be contrasted only with the help of others, anguished disorientation seems to withdraw from the 'public interpretative state', breaking the links that

---

10 Heidegger, *Being and Time*, pp. 181–2.

bind the individual to the anonymous and collective 'they' (*they* say this or that; *they* behave in such and such a way, etc.). At the mercy of an undefined dread—which is, however, capable of taking his breath away—is the person who finds himself alone outside of the 'common home'. And yet, when *every* form of life experiences, or even presupposes, the 'not-being-at-home' as a simple phenomenal condition, nobody is less isolated—or closer to the 'Dasein-with of others'—than the one who immediately perceives the terrible pressure of an undetermined context.

The as yet nameless feeling that results from the complete coincidence of fear and anxiety is characterized by the unavoidable relation with the presence of the other; it is a matter that concerns *many* people [*molti*]; it even contributes to founding the very concept of *multitude*. The 'many' are effectively such insofar as they *share* the experience of 'not-being-at-home'. This experience shatters every fictional 'common home', crushes its foul familiarity, and upsets the 'environmental' forms of protection derived from the inclusion in the *ethnos* and *demos*. However, as we will see, the 'not-being-at-home'—the state of mind of the multitude—annihilates the parodic communion of the 'home' only because it highlights what is really *common*; and, better, only because it exposes us to the Common as such. Against what Heidegger thinks, the radical disorientation withdraws us from the deceitful appearance of 'my owned self' and delivers us to a 'public interpretative state' in which *they* lose themselves or *they* save themselves. The exacerbated precariousness of the 'many' opens the possibility of a *public sphere*. I will later return to this point.

Thirdly—and perhaps most importantly—we must call into question the very couple: dread/shelter; or better, the presumed possibility of breaking it up into two distinct terms, where one is the premise and the other the conclusion. Believing that we first perceive the world-context as an unbearable dangerousness and only subsequently devote ourselves to devising a protective network is an optical illusion. The risk inherent in belonging to a shapeless and always potential context is never perceived as such, in the pure state, or preliminarily. On the contrary, this risk is manifested only because we are always already busy with circumscribing and mitigating it. We notice the surrounding threat as well as our vulnerability only insofar as we have *reacted* by adopting this or that strategy of reassurance. Rigorously, we should not even speak of a 'reaction'; any further reference to a chronological sequence or a cause-effect relation is misleading. There is no danger-stimulus and shelter-response. Rather, the search for protection constitutes the original and indivisible experience in which, by elaborating an antidote, we manage to glimpse something evil.

Moreover, the world's undetermined dangerousness is not only revealed *in* the always already ongoing attempt to find a shelter, but also fully expressed *as* the shelter that is attained time after time. Ultimately, the authentic risk amounts to certain ways of responding to the omnilateral riskiness of the vital context (for example, by relying on the sovereign, or nourishing the nightmare of a racist 'little nation', or ensconcing oneself in professional success, etc.). Only a certain way of confronting anxiety, or better, of matching up to the feeling of common contingency (for instance, through the obsessive care of 'my owned self' that 'discloses Dasein as *"solus ipse"*'), is properly anguished. The unrealizable *dynamis* of the world-context is a source of both threat and protection; however, this ambivalence becomes obvious only in the contrast between different strategies of reassurance; the behaviour meant to provide a shelter turns out to be dangerous *or* redemptive. The couple dread/shelter is therefore resolved in the alternative between antithetical forms of 'safety' (and this alternative is always articulated anew by political action). What is truly protective is the shelter that shields us from *dreadful protections*.

4.3 THE UNCANNY

Here I will use the term *uncanny* in order to specify the feeling in which fear and anxiety not only merge but also blend and become indistinguishable. My choice of this keyword has little or nothing to do with the meanings Freud attributes to it in the well-known essay *Das Unheimliche*.[11] I rather maintain its ordinary use, according to which the uncanny is a particular event (for instance, the appearance of a ghost or the failed recognition of oneself in the mirror) that, however, throws us into a state of utter confusion, calls into question our relation with the world as a whole, and makes the latter undecipherable and terrifying. With a certain amount of lexical opportunism, I avail myself of such a habitual meaning to introduce the concept of dread that—indifferent to ghosts and mirrors—concerns in general the ethical situation in which there is no longer a credible demarcation between factual risk and absolute unsafety. Reciprocally, I term *ease* the feeling-sheltered that circumvents and dismisses every 'sublime' distinction between an empirical protection (guaranteed by communities that are equally stable and 'poor-in-world') and the unconditioned immunity from the 'sensuous part of our being' (which instead would be accorded by the transcendent moral law).

However, I said earlier that the real danger is itself manifested *as* a shelter. Radical dread (or rather, more precisely, the kind of dread in which fear and anxiety become completely indiscernible) is inspired by certain defences from the world—certain horrifying free zones. Now, affirming that the genesis of the uncanny lies in the very search for protection comes very close, at least at first sight, to Freud's approach. My initial lexical opportunism seems to give way to a substantial consonance. But this only seems to be the case. To clarify this point, it is worth sketching out the thesis exposed in *Das Unheimliche*.

---

11 Sigmund Freud, 'The Uncanny' in James Strachey (ed.), *The Standard Edition of the Complete Psychological Works of Sigmund Freud*, VOL. 27 (London: Vintage, 2001[1919]).

It goes without saying that what follows is not a real investigation, but a rhetorical device whose aim is to qualify a concept by means of a contrast.

According to Freud, the feeling of the uncanny is connected with 'the constant recurrence of the same thing', that is, with *repetition*.[12] When we come across the number 62 several times in a single day, we may be overwhelmed by an unsayable apprehension if we recognize in that number an indication of the span of life allotted to us. Another occasion of panic is generated by the duplication of our self by means of a doppelganger—the 'double' threatens the identity of the ego, usurping its character and destiny. We are also seized by an obscure worry when, having wandered around for some time, we unexpectedly find ourselves back at the same place we intended to leave. Considerable trepidation is similarly caused by the too frequent materialization of what we thought in secret. But these different forms of iteration, whose current trait is that they terrify us, used to have in the past—in long gone phases of civilization or in early infancy—an apotropaic function. That is, they offered a protection from chance and unexpected events, by averting or subduing the destructive forces of the universe. The ultimate doppelganger was the immortal soul; the reappearance of the same number established a comforting regularity; the periodic return to the starting point guaranteed a principle of orientation. Freud's conclusion is well known; the uncanny does not correspond to the unusual but to 'that class of the frightening which leads back to what is known of old and long familiar'.[13] More precisely, what perturbs[14] us is the unexpected re-emergence of the repetition that used to be apotropaic, but which

---

12 Freud, 'The Uncanny', p. 234.

13 Freud, 'The Uncanny', p. 220.

14 The reader should here bear in mind that '*das Unheimliche*' is translated into Italian as '*il perturbante*', literally, 'that which perturbs' [Trans.].

was later *repressed* (if it concerned infancy) or *overcome* (if it had to do with archaic times).

This outline suffices to specify, by contrast, the use of the term 'uncanny' as an *ethical* category. In Freud, the temporal succession is decisive; the primitive shelter presents itself again with a sinister appearance because it was dismissed and forgotten, that is, because at a certain moment it stopped being a shelter. Instead, when I speak here of *dreadful protections*, I am referring to the frightening character that pertains to certain strategies of reassurance that are more *current* and effective than ever. The transformation of safety into a threat is not diachronic, does not hinge on the gap between past and present, and does not presuppose an intermediate phase in which what is well known and familiar is concealed by repression. On the contrary, the risk consists of what carries out an apotropaic function precisely and only now; *insofar as* it carries it out; for the *way in which* it carries it out. At times, what produces an unbearable apprehension is the well known on which we did not cease to rely; that is to say, the well known as not repressed, more than ever exposed to our gaze, and impossible to ignore.

On this basis, we can formulate a more suitable definition of the two keywords I introduced earlier. I call *uncanny* the acute threat emanating from the shelters we currently attend, that is, the danger that originates from some reactions to the dangerousness of the world-context. I call *ease* the protection from the uncanny, that is, the *second-degree shelter* that safeguards us from destructive shelters. If you wish, ease is the form of reassurance with regard to the world-context, when the latter's riskiness is manifested first and foremost in the terrifying apotropaic practices adopted to appease it. The opposition between the uncanny and ease is therefore unravelled as the opposition between alternative ways of defending ourselves from danger.

Let us consider again the crucial experience of repetition. According to Freud, the recurrence of the same number, which used to comfort us (was *heimlich*, or habitual), now dismays us (becomes *unheimlich*, sinister). But we saw that the ease and uncanny now at stake are not successive stages, but rather concurrent and contrary possibilities, which are juxtaposed to or cancel one another. We therefore have to think of two kinds of repetition that, articulating the same need for safety, nonetheless give rise to divergent outcomes. One kind of repetition is uncanny; the other adumbrates ease. They both unfold on the surface; they are simultaneous and even interactive; endowed with the same origin, and yet incompatible. Before returning to our main argument, we should embark upon a short digression concerning the apotropaic virtues of the 'Do it again!'.

4.4 DO IT AGAIN!

It is certainly the case that Walter Benjamin always remained interested in infancy. And it is equally uncontroversial that, with admirable timeliness, he established the crucial traits of the mechanical reproduction of the work of art. What has instead been overlooked is the very close connection between these two well-known facts. Benjamin immediately understood the new conditions of cultural production (photography, radio, cinema, etc.) *because* he did not preclude himself access to the experience of the child, and he drew from it important lessons on the fundamental tendencies of his time. It is only because he long dwelt on the play of children—characterized by the inexhaustible *iteration* of the same gestures—that he could comprehend the precise meaning of large-scale *seriality*—which is by now typical of not only cultural industry but also of every aspect of immediate experience. We in fact glimpse in this seriality the same demand for protection and orientation that guides the iterations of childhood.

Reviewing a book on toys, Benjamin writes words that could somehow also be applied to the inhabitants of a contemporary metropolitan city:

> We know that for a child the law of repetition is the soul of play, that nothing gives him greater pleasure than to 'Do it again!' [. . .]. 'All things would be resolved in a trice / if we could only do them twice.' Children act on this proverb of Goethe. Except that the child is not satisfied with twice, but wants the same thing again and again, a hundred or even a thousand times. This is not only the way to master frightening fundamental experiences—by deadening one's own response, by arbitrarily conjuring up experiences, or through parody; it also means enjoying one's victories and triumphs over and over again, with total intensity. An adult relieves his heart from its terrors and doubles happiness by turning it into a story. A child creates the entire event anew and starts again right from the beginning. Here, perhaps, is the deepest explanation for the two meanings of the German word *Spielen* ['to play' and 'to perform']: the element of repetition is what is actually common to them. Not a 'doing as if' but a 'doing the same thing over and over again', the transformation of a shattering experience into habit—that is the essence of play.[15]

The drive to 'do it again', which is typical of infancy, lies also at the origins of mechanically reproducible experience. In both cases, we attempt to free our mind from terror. This observation might already have prevented Benjamin from indulging in a nostalgic regret for previous forms of production and reception of the work of art; insofar as a primary and insuppressible need seems to be appeased by reproducibility, it is useless to bear a grudge against it. The actual question is rather: Why does the society of advanced capitalism

---

15 Walter Benjamin, 'Toys and Plays' in *Selected Writings: Volume 2, Part 1, 1927–1930* (Cambridge, MA: Harvard University Press, 2005), p. 120.

resume a characteristic trait of infancy? What do they share? The answer is to be sought in the absence of solid habits capable of absorbing the blows of chance, treading a path into the undetermined, and domesticating contingence. The child and the inhabitant of a metropolitan city are equally devoid of tradition and without bearings. Deprived of the shelter provided by a 'custom', they both confide in repetition in order to protect themselves from the shocks of the unexpected and find some form of orientation.

The ludic iteration of tender age has always been deemed to show that there are as *yet* no habits but that, as a matrix, it paves the way for their acquisition. This is no longer the case. Far from being preparatory, the preliminary stage has become permanent. Adult experience remains repetitive and habitualness does not follow. Benjamin speaks instead of a general 'poverty of experience' that forces us to 'start from scratch; to make a new start; to make a little go a long way'.[16] The child's apotropaic iteration does not give way to the much more sophisticated shelter of *ethos* and communitarian traditions, resurfacing from time to time as a 'repressed' uncanny. On the contrary, the original 'do it again' is *irremovable*, and persists as highlighted. For this reason—given that we never stop collectively resorting to its typical form of protection—infancy should be considered as a category of public spirit. It is neither a preamble nor an apprenticeship, but a critical *paradigm* capable of throwing further light on the social relations and ethical conducts of late modernity.

However, the analogy between the 'law of repetition', on which the child relies, and mechanical reproduction conceals a radical contrast; in the end, it is reversed into an irreconcilable disagreement. Within the same search for safety both the possibility of the *uncanny* and that of *ease* are delineated; these are synchronic but opposite possibilities.

---

16 Walter Benjamin, 'Experience and Poverty' in *Selected Writings: Volume 2, Part 2, 1931–34*, p. 732.

The metropolitan forms of life, devoid of traditions and poor of experience, show puerile traits that—in spite of forcefully summoning infancy as their explanatory key—convey only a degraded, and at times appalling, image of it. The society of advanced capitalism brandishes the 'do it again' in order to build a nightmarish kindergarten. Mechanical reproduction opposes the *compulsion to repeat* typical of commodities and wage-labour to ludic repetition. Cultural industry embellishes the 'poverty of experience' so that it may pass unobserved; it protects from the absence of habits, selling bare iteration as their surrogate; establishes surreptitious 'traditions' that are nevertheless binding; and surrounds the compulsive revival of the same gesture with an 'aura'. Its demerit is not ruining our souls, but, on the contrary, preserving them at all costs and despite everything.

The antidote to the *uncanny puerility* of the society of spectacle lies in the seriousness of infancy. The child that demands to listen to the same story, or grab the same toy, perceives at each turn what is the same as unique. Each replication has the value of a prototype, a milestone, and an *experimentum crucis* (as Benjamin writes, it is not 'a "doing as if" but a "doing the same thing over and over again"'). The 'once and for all' dwells precisely in the 'do it again'; every single iteration is irreversible and loaded with a heart-breaking contingency; it aspires at a sort of ephemeral perfection; and exhibits uniqueness devoid of any aura. The child's ludic activity evokes the possibility of ease because, instead of childishly dissimulating the 'poverty of experience', it gives it utmost relevance, inhabits it, and tries to obtain from it an appeasement or at least 'something decent'.[17] In the age in which such poverty has become the rule, this elementary activity acquires for the first time a *historical* resonance. That is, it refers back to a public praxis, which is finally able to seize the opportunities inherent to the unavoidable 'not-being-at-home'. We could say that since every communitarian *ethos* has conflagrated and there is no

---

17 Benjamin, 'Experience and Poverty', p. 733.

longer any trace of habits, political action is obliged to resume the peculiar connection between repetition and contingency, 'do it again' and 'once and for all' that characterizes the *Spiel* of infancy. Not unlike the incoming human being, the one who acts in a public sphere himself glimpses in the eternal return of the same the most propitious occasion—or, rather, the only one he is granted—to start something that is truly new.

4.5 COMMON PLACES AND THE PUBLIC CHARACTER OF THE MIND

The materialist interpretation of the dynamical sublime, that is, of 'the state in which one says to oneself "I am safe, nothing can happen to me, whatever happens"', still needs to take the most challenging step—locating the shared lineage from which both the uncanny and ease derive. For the time being, we know that this bipolarity expresses the danger and protection inherent to the relation with the world in general (where—it is important to stress—such a relation emerges, in all its ambivalence, only in the always already ongoing attempt to protect oneself from the world itself). We therefore only know that both the uncanny and ease have to do with that 'not-being-at-home' in which we experience the immediate pressure of an amorphous and undetermined context—and defend ourselves from it in the most different ways. This is not enough. A state of disorientation and constant vulnerability does not explain as such the development of opposite strategies of reassurance. We still lack a decisive middle term. In order to identify it, we need to ask what the salient phenomenon is in which the 'not-being-at-home' manifests itself.

The phrases 'poverty of experience' and 'not-being-at-home'—which are equivalent—designate a mode of being by stressing the 'no longer', that is, an incurred loss. We must instead point out the convex side and the content in high relief of the mode of being in question. More precisely, I refer here to the 'not-being-at-home' as a situation that bonds [*accomuna*] a multitude, makes the 'Dasein-with of others' unavoidable, and effectively discloses a 'public interpretative state'. What is, in fact, the meaning of the repetition in which—for want of anything better—those who are poor of experience and homeless confide? In repetition, everything that, in a given vital field, is known, shared, and *common* coalesces and clearly shows itself. However, this common-known is not familiar; it does not at all resemble a tradition or habit. Moreover, repetition—the heraldic symbol of poor experience—does not limit itself to separating what is common from what is usual, but affirms the former to the detriment of the latter. The communality exhibited by the 'do it again' has the curious prerogative of abolishing every kind of viscous familiarity. What is, then, its content?

To get a sense of it, let us consider the role Aristotle assigns to the 'common places' (*topoi koinoi*) in his treatise on rhetoric.[18] They are not banalities or stereotypes, but the basic linguistic forms and argumentative structures that pertain to every discourse, independently from their theme and the occasion on which they are uttered. They are actually so basic that they constitute the unnoticed presupposition of discourse in general. By way of example, Aristotle mentions three *topoi koinoi*: the opposition of contraries, the more and less, and the relationship of reciprocity. As we can see, it is a matter of intellectual functions that are nearly indispensable and concern the very possibility of reasoning. We could say that the 'common places' incorporate the potency of the intellect; they are nothing other than the *places of the mind*. And, vice versa, the life of the mind, insofar as it is concentrated in 'places' that everybody shares, shows that it is *common*. But this commonality remains hidden or neglected as long as experience is, so to speak, *rich* in habitual customs. In Aristotle's treatise, the 'common places' do not have an autonomous consistence, since they are only the inconspicuous connective texture of the 'proper' or 'special' spaces (*topoi idioi*). The latter group

---

18 Aristotle, *Rhetoric* 1358a.

together arguments, inferences, metaphors, values, and jokes that suit one or the other particular discursive situation (the Forum or the Academy, the workplace or the party's local offices, etc.). All in all, the 'proper places' follow the fragmented articulation of the communitarian *ethos*, and isolate what belongs exclusively to each field. The predominance of the 'proper places' and the ancillary invisibility of the 'common' ones provide us with the typical ethical-rhetorical hierarchy of which we will now have to acknowledge the reversal.

The poverty of experience is actually characterized by the *superabundance of world*, that is, a non-reduced relationship with the raw and undetermined context of existence. The superabundance of world is what empties out and atrophies the 'proper places', around which stable roles, lasting identities, and familiar customs were located. This superabundance is also what moves the *topoi koinoi* to the foreground, where they themselves become the decisive thematic repertoire. The generic potency of the mind as illustrated by the 'common places' constitutes in fact the only source of protection from the world-context, which is in turn always generic and formless. The utmost exposure to the world implies, as a reaction, the utmost proximity to the *places of the mind*—the *topoi koinoi*. In short, we should bear in mind two complementary aspects. First, experience is poor when it does not have any principle of orientation except for the pure intellect; this is an experience whose *topography* amounts only to abstract paradigms, bare logical functions, and extremely general categories (such as the opposition of contraries or the relationship of reciprocity). Second, inasmuch as the pure intellect stands for the only principle of orientation of poor experience, it gains a full and immediate visibility. The potency of the mind becomes, so to speak, external and *conspicuous*. The fact that it is a shared good—its typical commonality—is no longer a hidden presupposition, but the dazzling evidence that qualifies every discourse and action. In addition to being common, the intellect is also *public*.

The idea of a 'public intellect' seems rough and paradoxical because it contradicts a long tradition according to which thinking is a solitary activity, devoid of external manifestations, and as such alien to the care of common affairs. From Aristotle to Hannah Arendt, there is a widespread agreement on this point. However, there is at least one noticeable exception worth mentioning. The public character of the intellect—its irruption into the world of appearances—is outlined in a very suggestive way by Marx when he claims that 'the conditions of the process of social life itself have come under the control of the *general intellect* and been transformed in accordance with it.'[19] The expression 'general intellect' is perhaps a polemical rejoinder to Rousseau's *volonté générale*; or, more probably, a materialist echo of the *nous poietikos*, the active—separate and impersonal—intellect that Aristotle discusses in *On the Soul*.[20] In any case, the concept of general intellect, in Marx, designates the mind as an external and collective potency.

The mind is an external potency insofar as abstract knowledge becomes an 'immediate productive force', 'scientific capacity' is objectivized in the machine system, and entire conceptual constellations are as substantial and effective as material facts. It is also a collective potency; as Alfred Sohn-Rethel writes commenting on Marx, 'in this form, to use a juridical term, thought has the intellectual power of attorney [*pro cura*] over society. It literally thinks "for" society. Its functions have a direct social form.'[21] However, the notion of general intellect should not be reduced to the application of natural science to the process of production. What is in question is rather the conspicuousness or public character of pure thought itself,

---

19 Karl Marx, *Grundrisse* (Martin Nicolaus trans.) (available at: https://bit.ly/3PVJKyp; last accessed: 1 June 2022), Notebook 7: 'The Chapter on Capital'.

20 Aristotle, *On the Soul* 429a–430a.

21 Alfred Sohn-Rethel, *Geistige und körperliche Arbeit* (Frankfurt: Suhrkamp, 1970), p. 81.

as autonomous from given experiences and indifferent to particular applications. Moreover, we are not dealing with the *works* of thought but with the mere *aptitude* to think. Marx highlights and raises the generic potentialities of the mind to the level of public resource: the faculty of language, the predisposition to learning, the capacity of abstracting and correlating, and the inclination to self-reflection. 'General intellect' should be understood literally as an *intellect in general*.

What is the form of existence that is correlated to the public character of the mind? What is the *bios theoretikos*, or intellectual life, that corresponds to the general intellect? To solve this problem, it is useful to dwell on an ancient simile, assessing anew its scope and validity. In an early writing, the *Protrepticus*,[22] Aristotle compares the conduct of the thinker with the *bios xenikos*, the way of living of the foreigner. The philosopher behaves like an exile because he avoids public meetings, puts a damper on the plurality of dissonant voices one hears in the city, and minimises his interactions with the world. In order to access mental life—which is nonetheless extremely *common*—he must desert the political *community*, separating from the multitude of other men. It goes without saying that the very concept of 'public intellect' is opposed to such a representation of the *bios theoretikos*. But the fact is that it opposes it by still maintaining (and even developing beyond measure) the analogy between *bios theoretikos* and *bios xenikos*—between thinker and foreigner.

The commonality of the mind is not concealed but, as noticed, external and conspicuous. Each and every one of us draws on it in the presence of others, exposing himself to their gaze, and enjoying or suffering from their company. The commonality of the mind is thus manifested in public meetings; pertains to the city's fortunes; inspires this or that form of *acting in concert*, and different kinds of collective praxis. The intellectual life connected with the general intellect always concerns a multitude. And yet, who are the 'many'

---

22 Aristotle, *Protrepticus* B56.

who are responsible for the *bios theoretikos* (a *bios theoretikos* that in fact requires the 'Dasein-with of others' while it remains precluded to the '*solus ipse*')? Although its original meaning has been completely disrupted, the comparison established in the *Protrepticus* turns out to be equally adequate; the 'many' who participate in the general intellect are invariably *xenoi*, exiles, and foreigners. Better said, they are those who go through the emotional condition of 'not-being-at-home'.

To confirm this, we just need to reverse the order of our exposition, and directly start with this emotional condition. The 'not-being-at-home' is the state of mind that characterizes the *bios xenikos*, the life of the exile. In order to orient themselves in the world, foreigners can only confide in the *topoi koinoi*—the basic functions of thought. As we know, the 'common places', to which every kind of reliable bearing leads, coincide with the *places of the mind*. Therefore, those who do not feel at home, the *xenoi*, constantly live in proximity to the intellect, and have a propensity for a sort of *bios theoretikos*. Reversing the direction of the simile, we could say that exiles behave like thinkers, and that the *bios xenikos* shows a great affinity with the *bios theoretikos*. However, a radical difference emerges here with regard to Aristotle's setting; living in proximity to the intellect, the exile does not obtain the *autarcheia*, or self-sufficiency, but is instead related with his many counterparts, and attains a 'public interpretative state'.

The crucial point is that, while the *bios xenikos*, discussed by Aristotle, applies to an exceptional and temporary condition (the foreigner has a fatherland to which he can return; the thinker can reconnect with the communitarian *ethos* of the city), the 'not-being-at-home' is instead an unavoidable and irreversible mode of being; that is to say, a mode of being of the *many*. Insofar as they are never provided with genuine 'proper places', the homeless do not even have to decide whether to attend them (thus adhering to associated life) or separate from them (like the philosopher and the exile). Rather, they always already share, as a crowd, the places of the mind; they always already resort to the potency of the intellect—in reciprocal agreement or contrast—in order to confront the contingency of the world-context and mitigate the grip of precariousness. For this reason, the places of the mind resonate with the murmur of the multitude. For this reason, the potency of the intellect resembles a *common musical score*, which each and every one plays in public, or better, before the 'public' made of the other foreigners. In the end, for this reason, the *bios xenikos* is a form of *political existence*.

4.6 THE SPACE OF THE INTELLECT

The aim of the last few pages was to identify the source from which both anguished risk—which I call the 'uncanny'—and comforting safety—which I call 'ease'—originate. I said that this source—which is unitary but ambivalent—is located in the state of mind of 'not-being-at-home'. But, in order to recover it, it is not enough to refer to disorientation as a condition of excruciating vulnerability and mere indigence. In fact, insofar as the uncanny and ease are nothing other than opposite strategies of reassurance, their common matrix must consist of a basic form of protection, which is as such still undecided. It was therefore necessary to focus on the primary shelter that the very 'not-being-at-home' never fails to formulate, that is, go back to the ways in which disorientation already replies to the ominousness of the world and alleviates its pressure. In other words, it was a matter of considering the 'not-being-at-home' starting from the apotropaic resource that it uncovers. This is what we just discussed in terms of the *topoi koinoi*, the general intellect, and the peculiar *bios theoretikos* that pertains to a multitude of exiles.

The 'not-being-at-home' highlights, or better, *publicizes* what is effectively common: the potency of the intellect and the life of the mind. The public intellect amounts to the main shelter from a vital context that is always raw and potential. It is indeed an apotropaic resource. But, by protecting us from the contingency of the sensible world, the intellect also introjects its ambivalence and reproduces it on an ethical level; it is itself presented, at the same time, as the 'last condition' of danger and as a source of safety. The apotropaic apparatuses that, deriving from it, articulate the preliminary defence offered by the life of the mind turn out to be, at any given time, supremely threatening or really redeeming. The general intellect is therefore the unitary lineage from which both the uncanny and ease originate.

Saying that thought is external, enmeshed in the world of appearances, and relevant to a multitude, means hinting at its possible relationship with space. But is it legitimate to even suppose such a relationship? Can we seriously discuss the *spatiality of the pure intellect*? Answering affirmatively to this kind of question is perhaps the badge of honour of materialist reflection. Moreover, it is only when we closely examine the juncture of the general intellect with space (or, rather the inhibition or the unfolding of this juncture) that we manage to grasp the actual distinction between the uncanny and ease. It is only in this way that we can clarify how the general intellect itself—which safeguards and shelters us—can at times become lethal and unleash a panic fear.

The potency of the mind has a pervasive and ubiquitous nature (like the *topoi koinoi* in which it is condensed)—it can never be situated in a specific 'where'. It goes without saying that thought does not occupy a place *in* space. However, it can establish its own spatiality. The public intellect is not 'here' or 'there' or 'between' two things, but can generate some peculiar kinds of 'here', 'there', and 'between'. It is in no place, yet it can nonetheless *give place*. If the public intellect always seems to be so close, this is not because it is located at a minimal distance, but because it can itself open a space at the heart of which proximities and distances are delineated. This further (and possible) space is not metric but *political*. That is, we are dealing with the context in which the 'many' (the *xenoi* and homeless) act and distinguish themselves, gather or separate, take decisions and look after common affairs. In the end, this is the context in which the 'many' fully assert their being-many by tracing positions, trajectories, and crossroads in it. The general intellect spatially becomes extrinsic as a political community of exiles and as a Republic of the multitude. But this process of becoming extrinsic is only a possibility. It may *not* happen. If it does not happen, the public intellect takes on a threatening appearance.

What perturbs us is precisely the failed spatialization of the general intellect. The latter is, in this case, well conveyed by the words Heidegger uses to describe anguished danger: 'It is so near that it is oppressive and takes away one's breath—and yet it is nowhere.'[23] If it is not fulfilled, the spatializing inclination of the general intellect—its power to *give place*—is in fact perceived as an *atopian proximity*, which is equally enigmatic and frightening. Let us explain this point in more detail. The *commonality* of the intellect strikes fear, or better causes absolute unsafety, when it is not—spatially—translated into an autonomous *political community*—although it remains a 'productive force', that is, the irrevocable (and atopian) precondition of the social process of labour. The *public* character of the mind is distressing when it does not give rise to a *public sphere*, that is, a context in which the actions and discourses of the multitude are inscribed, but figures as a centripetal apodictic potency, which is always again transfused into the administrative apparatuses of the States. The uncanny amounts to a commonality without a political community and a public character without a public sphere. Against what tedious small talk has long claimed, panic fear is not the consequence of a fracture between individual biography and the impersonal potencies that sustain society; on the contrary, it arises precisely from the calamitous inherence of the individual to the general intellect—or better, from an inherence that is calamitous because it is devoid of a spatial organization.

---

23 Heidegger, *Being and Time*, p. 180.

What kind of jeopardy and fright does a commonality without a community (or, which is the same, a public character without a public sphere) entail? Provided that we grant only metaphorical value to it, there is a passage in Freud that helps us to sketch an answer. Among the various forms in which the uncanny is manifested, following the suggestion of a patient, Freud includes also the supposed 'omnipotence of thought'.[24] The certainty that thoughts are able to acquire an independent life and realize themselves with very concrete consequences is truly sinister and terrifying. This belief is inspired by archaic (or childhood) animism—the idea that bestows on psychic forces the capacity to influence the course of events and prevent danger. But if it is resurrected in a fully civilized age (or in adulthood), instead of being reassuring, animism dismays us. The reason for that is easy to guess. Thanks to the extrinsic power of the intellect—its immediate material effect—anybody can harm us, strike at us, and subject us. As soon as it becomes conspicuous, the life of the mind dangerously obliterates distances, produces a disquieting amalgamation with others, and exposes us to the plurality of our counterparts.

The general intellect gives an objective texture to the 'omnipotence of thoughts'. Unlike the phobias examined by Freud, what is thus at stake is not the belated resumption of an obsolete (and illusory) apotropaic practice, but a protection from the world that is fully effective and more topical than ever. And yet, if its commonality does not become extrinsic in a public sphere, the general intellect perturbs us in a way similar to the resurgence of animism. Just as physical space makes the *multiple* possible, so the space of the intellect is the condition on which the political existence of the *multitude* depends. If such a condition is lacking, the 'many' are brought together in a sort of symbiotic connection, which is far from innocuous. Associated by the power of the mind, but devoid of a field in which to act and separate from one another, the 'many' sketch out relationships that are not too dissimilar from those existing among the participants of

24 Freud, 'The Uncanny', p. 240.

a séance. These relationships are viscous, uncontrollable, and centripetal. They are divested of spatiality as the most important mundane prerogative—and thus characterized by the *loss of world*. As extrinsic yet non-spatial, the general intellect protects us from the ominousness of the world-context, but it deprives the bonds among the members of our species of a context, that is, of a world. And this privation is, in turn, extraordinarily threatening. The connection that each of the 'many' has with the presence of the other is permeated with fear.

On the one hand, the *sharing* of generic communicative and cognitive skills becomes the actual foundation of every kind of praxis, starting with that of labour. Hence every form of concerted action (and socialization) based on a preliminary *division*—for instance, the technical division of labour—is contracted. However, on the other hand, if the sharing of the intellect remains non-spatialized—that is, *impolitical*—it favours a direct subjection, no longer mediated by roles and mansions. Symbiotic communality is marked by arbitrary yet vigorous hierarchies, and constipated by meticulous bonds; actually, it itself constitutes the presupposition for their continuous proliferation. The unavoidable relationship with the presence of the other, implied by the public character of the mind, shows itself as the universal restoration of *personal dependence*. 'Personal' has here two meanings: we depend on this or that person, not on rules endowed with an anonymous coercive power; the entire person is subjugated, that is, the simple aptitude for thinking and acting, and all in all the 'generic existence' of everyone (to use the expression with which Marx designates the experience of the individual that mirrors in itself and paradigmatically exhibits the basic faculties of humankind). The impolitical sharing of the general intellect brings with it an uncanny 'being at the mercy of'. We are at the mercy of those with whom we are associated; hazardously exposed to what associates us; and endangered precisely by the commonality that nonetheless could save us.

Ease is the state of mind that takes over when we manage to hold the uncanny back. It is the feeling of safety that emerges from having eluded or defeated atrocious strategies of reassurance; from having contrasted certain ways of facing anxiety that are truly distressing. As I already said, ease consists of having a *second-degree shelter*, which protects us from the *dreadful protections* elaborated to thwart the dangers related to the 'sensuous part of our being'. This kind of shelter preserves us from those apotropaic practices in which the unbearable threatening character of the surrounding world is, on the one hand, curbed, yet, on the other, re-emerges in a new guise with more violence and even reaches its apex. These definitions are as such still too simple, yet they have been gaining some determined contents. In fact, we now know what are the terrifying refuges to which the second-degree shelter is opposed—and which alone can put us at ease. Let us succinctly recall them: the communality that is not spatially articulated, and hence *symbiotic*, of the intellect; the 'loss of world', which characterizes the *viscous* relationship with the presence of the other; an *impolitical* sharing of the potency of thought, from which there follows a proliferation of surreptitious hierarchical bonds, based on personal dependence. The nature of danger announces what an adequate defence should be.

Ease feeds on the same source that nourishes the uncanny: commonality and the public character of the intellect. Ease returns to the origin of risk, for the simple reason that this origin is its own origin. It hinges on what often appears to be threatening and at times becomes lethal. It does not transcend the 'last condition under which danger can be presented for us',[25] but inhabits it and, so to speak, takes possession of it, deriving reassuring consequences from it. I call ease the spatialization of the general intellect—and thus, the conversion of its sharing into a political community, and the unfolding of its public character into a public sphere. The *political* sharing of the

---

25 Schiller, *Of the Sublime.*

life of the mind is indeed that second-degree shelter which awards us a non-insignificant (and, in turn, non-frightening) safety. The possibility that the potency of thought may become extrinsic like a political space, or better, as the Republic of the multitude, is perhaps a plausible materialist transcription of the instance of protection inherent to the dynamical sublime.

Moreover, the public sphere of the intellect is not an eventuality among others, but the dividing line that obliges us to rethink anew the major themes which modern political philosophy has elaborated, namely, obedience, democracy, hostility, violence, and the state of exception. For example, it suffices to mention the transformation the concept of the multitude undergoes here. This concept (by means of which Hobbes intended to flag up the utmost threat to the State, and Spinoza the source of freedom) can never be disconnected from that of unity—which is symmetrical to it. The 'many' nevertheless necessitate the 'one', that is, a *quid* that associates them. Thus, it all rests on defining *what* the unifying principle is. For Hobbes—but also for the socialist-democratic tradition—such a principle is the State. And yet, as soon as the multitude is subjected to the 'supreme power', instead of finding cohesion, it simply ceases to be what it is, and is transformed into its contrary, namely, the people—of which, according to Hobbes, we must say that it is 'a *single* entity, with *a single will*'.[26] The usual concept of the multitude is therefore negative or interstitial, and is only helpful in indicating the disorder that precedes the institution of the State, or the uprisings that accompany its periodic crises. The situation changes, and even becomes completely different, as soon as we realize that the nexus between the 'many' consists of their common participation in the potency of the mind. From this angle, the multitude is not a cloud of particles that *still* lacks unity, but a lasting form of political existence that is affirmed

---

26 Thomas Hobbes, *On the Citizen* (Cambridge: Cambridge University Press, 1998 [1642]), p. 137.

starting from a 'one'—the public intellect—radically heterogeneous to the State. Unity is not a conclusion but an *incipit*; the multitude is a result and not a presupposition. The 'many' never converge into a *volonté générale*, because they already share a general intellect. Persisting as 'many', they call into question the further persistence of that 'monopoly on political decision-making'[27] which is called State. The public sphere of the intellect erodes and unbalances the very foundation of statehood. But it should be clear that all this is only a summary allusion to a set of issues whose examination would require a separate book.

Finally, we need to specify the relationship between the concept of public sphere—that is, ease—and the other aspects of the idea of world (in order to fully highlight the cosmological meaning of this sphere, that is, its contribution to a *cosmologia rationalis* that is not at all metaphysical). In Wittgensteinian terms, the problem would be the following: What is the juncture that connects the feeling of absolute *safety* to the feeling of *wonder* at the existence of the world? In Kantian terms, the question would be: What is the point of confluence, or even the indistinction, between the dynamical sublime (the superiority of the moral Self over mundane dangers) and the mathematical sublime (considering the world as an 'entirely given totality')? However, the arguments we presented in this essay impose a different formulation of the same problem. What is now at stake is the unity, and the reciprocal reference, between the perception of the *sensible context* and belonging to a *political context*.

The experience of the *public sphere* is akin to the experience of *raw nature*—it follows and even redoubles it. Like amorphous matter, which embraces us from all sides as a *continuum* that is not decomposable into discrete unities, the public sphere is itself 'all around' and never 'in front' of us. While the former is perceived out

---

27 Carl Schmitt, *Der Begriff des Politischen: Text vom 1932 mit einem Vorwort und drei Corollarien* (Berlin: Dunker & Humblot, 1963), p. 10.

of the corner of one's eye, the latter asserts itself—in a fully symmetrical way—in the omnilateral exhibition of the individual to the gaze of others (of the multitude that constitutes the unfailing 'all around' of anyone who embarks into a political action). Both raw nature and the public sphere have uncertain contours, and perpetually remain unfocused and opaque, superseding every kind or representation. Neither of the two is something 'entirely given', since in both cases we instead deal with an always and only *potential* context: the formless sensible is the 'flesh of the possible'; the public sphere is the potency of the intellect. The analogy also holds negatively. Just as infinite regression (caused by the thought of the world as an 'absolute whole') distorts and obscures the perception of the material context, so the failed spatialization of the general intellect inhibits the formation of a political context. Publicness without the public sphere theoretically corresponds to the endless backwards flight with which we try in vain to seize the world in its 'entire magnitude'.

The cosmological meaning of the public sphere therefore consists of *redoubling the experience of the world* that is always already accomplished in relation to raw nature. When we earlier claimed that ease does not transcend the 'last condition' of danger, but inhabits it and takes possession of it—to the point of turning it into a shelter—we implicitly referred to such a redoubling. In other words, we were referring to the *ethical-political repetition of the sensible context* carried out by the intellect, whose potency becomes spatially extrinsic as a public sphere. This ethical-political repetition of the experience of the world transforms *wonder* into *safety*.

VIRTUOSITY AND REVOLUTION

THE POLITICAL THEORY OF EXODUS

1.

Action, Labour, Intellect

Today, nothing seems so enigmatic—and unattainable—as acting. We could say in jest that if nobody asks me what political action is, I believe I know it; but if I have to explain it to somebody who asks, that supposed knowledge is reduced to inarticulate nonsense. And yet, what notion is more familiar than action in common language? Why is something obvious now cloaked in mystery and surprising? In order to answer this question, it is not enough to rally the usual host of indisputable ready-made explanations—unfavourable power relations, the persistent echo of the defeats we suffered, the arrogant resignation that postmodern ideology does not stop fomenting. Of course, all this matters, but does not explain anything by itself. Actually, it is confusing, since it makes us believe that we are going through a dark tunnel at the end of which everything will be back to normal. Instead, the paralysis of acting is connected with some essential aspects of contemporary experience. It is there, close to these aspects, that we need to delve into—knowing that they do not amount to an unfortunate conjuncture, but to an inescapable background. In order to break the spell, it is necessary to elaborate a model of action that will enable it to feed on precisely what is now blocking it. The interdiction itself is to be transformed into a *laissez-passer.*

According to a long tradition, the field of political action can be identified easily by drawing two boundaries. The first refers to *labour,* its instrumental and taciturn character, and that automatism that turns it into a repetitive and predictable process. The second refers to *pure thought* and its solitary and inconspicuous disposition. Unlike labour, political action intervenes on social relations, not on natural materials; it has to cope with what is possible and unexpected; political action modifies the context in which it is inscribed instead of enriching it with new objects. Unlike intellectual reflection, action is public and entrusted to exteriority, contingency, and the murmur of the multitude. This is what a long tradition teaches us. But, at the same time, we can no longer rely on this. The usual boundaries between Intellect, Labour, and Action (or, if you prefer to use Aristotle's jargon, *episteme, poiesis* and *praxis*) have been breached, and infiltrations and bridgeheads can be observed everywhere.

In the present notes, I will argue that: a) Labour has assimilated the distinctive traits of political action; b) this annexation has been made possible by the collusion between contemporary production and an Intellect that has become *public,* and as such has irrupted into the world of appearances. Ultimately, the eclipse of Action was caused by the symbiosis of Labour with the general intellect, or 'general social knowledge', which, according to Marx, transforms 'the process of social life itself'.[1] I will subsequently put forward two

---

[1] The full passage containing the expression 'general intellect' reads as follows: 'The development of fixed capital indicates to what degree general social knowledge has become a direct force of production, and to what degree, hence, the conditions of the process of social life itself have come under the control of the general intellect and been transformed in accordance with it. To what degree the powers of social production have been produced, not only in the form of knowledge, but also as immediate organs of social practice, of the real life process' (Karl Marx, *Grundrisse,* Notebook 7).

hypotheses: 1) The public and mundane character of thought—the material potency of the general intellect—amounts to the unavoidable starting point needed to redefine political praxis, as well as its salient problems—decision, government, democracy, violence, etc. In short, the alliance between Intellect and Action is to be opposed to that between Intellect and Labour. 2) While the symbiosis of knowledge with production offers an extreme, anomalous, and yet vigorous legitimation for the pact of obedience to the State, the junction between the general intellect and political Action enables us to glimpse the possibility of a *non-State public sphere.*

2.

Activity without Work

The dividing line between Labour and Action, which had been unstable and uncertain for long, finally disappeared altogether. According to Hannah Arendt (whose positions I would like to critically challenge here, and even oppose), this hybridization is due to the fact that modern political praxis has internalized the model of Labour, increasingly resembling a swift *manufacturing* whose 'product' is, at each turn, history, the State, the party, and so on.[1] This diagnosis should be overturned. What matters the most is not that political action is conceived as a production, but that production includes in itself many of the qualities of political action. In the post-Fordist age, it is Labour that looks like Action—in terms of unpredictability, the capacity to start something new, linguistic improvising, and the ability to cope with alternative possibilities. However, the fatal consequence of this is that, with respect to a Labour loaded with 'actionist' requirements, the passage to Action is presented as a *deterioration*, or at best a superfluous *duplication*. For the most part, it appears to be a deterioration; structured according to a rudimental logic of means/ends, politics

---

1 Hannah Arendt, *The Human Condition* (Chicago: The University of Chicago Press, 1998), section 31.

offers a communicative network and a content of knowledge that are poorer than those implemented in the current productive process. Being less complex than Labour and too similar to it, Action appears in any case as not so desirable.

2.1

In 'Results of the Immediate Process of Production' (and also, in almost identical words, in *Theories of Surplus Value*), Marx analyses intellectual labour by distinguishing two main kinds. On the one hand, there is the immaterial activity that 'results in commodities which exist separately from the producer [. . .] books, paintings and all products of art as distinct from the artistic achievement of the practising artist'.[2] On the other hand, we have to consider all those activities in which 'the product is not separable from the act of producing'—that is, those activities that find completion in themselves, without being objectivized in a work that supersedes them. The second type of intellectual labour is well exemplified by performing artists, for instance, a pianist or a dancer, but, more generally, it also includes all those whose work result in a *virtuoso performance*—orators, teachers, doctors or priests. Ultimately, this is a very wide range of human beings, encompassing everyone from Glenn Gould to the impeccable butler of many English novels.

Only the first of these two categories of intellectual labour fully fits with Marx's definition of 'productive labour' (which applies to work that creates surplus value, and not to merely useful or hard work). Virtuosos, who limit themselves to interpreting a score and do not leave lasting traces are, on the one hand, 'of microscopic significance when compared with the mass of capitalist production', yet, on the other, must also be regarded as 'wage-labour that is not at the same time productive labour'.[3] Whilst it is easy to understand

---

2 Karl Marx, *Capital*, VOL. 1 (London: Penguin, 1990), p. 1048.

3 Marx, *Capital*, VOL. 1, pp. 1044–5.

Marx's insistence on the quantitative irrelevance of virtuosos, his ver-
dict that they are 'unproductive' is somehow baffling. In principle,
there is no reason why the dancer could not give rise to surplus value.
But, for Marx, the point is that the absence of a work haunting the
world after the activity is over associates modern intellectual virtuosity with all those activities that offer a *personal service*; these activities are indeed unproductive insofar as in order to secure them one
has to spend revenues, and does not invest capital. The performing
artist, who is both subjugated and parasitic, finally falls into the limbo
of serf-labour.

The activities in which 'the product is not separable from the act
of producing' have a mercurial and ambiguous status, which is not
always and not completely grasped by the critique of political
economy. The reason for this difficulty is simple. Long before being
incorporated in capitalist production, virtuosity was the cornerstone
of ethics and politics. Moreover, it qualified Action as different from
(and even opposed to) Labour. Aristotle writes that 'the end of production is different from production, whereas that of action could
not be, since virtuous conduct is an end in itself.'[4] According to
Arendt:

> the performing arts [. . .] have indeed a strong affinity with
> politics. Performing artists—dancers, play-actors, musicians
> and the like—need an audience to show their virtuosity, just
> as acting men need the presence of others before whom they
> can appear; both need a publicly organized space for their
> 'work', and both depend upon others for the performance
> itself.[5]

---

4 Aristotle, *Nicomachean Ethics* 1139b.
5 Hannah Arendt, 'What Is Freedom?' in *The Portable Hannah Arendt* (New
York: Penguin, 2000), p. 446.

The pianist and the dancer stand precariously balanced on a watershed that divides divergent destinies; on the one hand, they may become examples of 'wage-labour that is not at the same time productive labour'; on the other, they allude to political action.[6] Their nature is amphibious. But so far each of the potential developments inherent to the figure of the performing artist—*poiesis* and *praxis*, Labour and Action—seems to exclude the opposite inclination. The status of the wage labourer is established to the detriment of political vocation, and vice versa. However, after a certain point, the alternative turns into a complicity, and the *aut . . . aut* is replaced by a paradoxical *et . . . et*; the virtuoso works (or rather is a worker *par excellence*) not despite but precisely because of the fact that his activity is very reminiscent of political praxis. The divergence comes to an end and, in this new situation, the antithetical investigations carried out by Marx and Arendt are of no help.

---

6 The fact that virtuosity is the conjoined twin of political action is clearly demonstrated *ex negativo* as soon as we pay attention to Glenn Gould's case. Gould was an extraordinary pianist who never tolerated an essential aspect of his activity, namely, public exposure, as well as the contingency and volatility of concerts. He obstinately tried to purge virtuosity of its inherent political character. He renounced performances, and claimed he was tired of . . . *vita activa* (an ancient phrase that designated participation in the sphere of public affairs, that is, politics). The most interesting fact is that, yearning for a sort of *impolitical virtuosity*, Gould was obliged to surreptitiously conceive his interpretations as a *work*. The refusal of the unpredictability and transience inherent to politics implies the necessity to anchor one's praxis to an external product. Gould thus took shelter in recording studios, relying on mechanical reproduction in the belief that the solitary making of a record stood at least as a surrogate of a life that does not need the 'presence of others', which, in total opposition to his being a virtuoso, he continued to crave.

2.2

In the post-Fordist productive organization, activity-without-work is no longer a special and problematic case and becomes the prototype of wage labour in general.

Here it is not worth recapitulating the detailed analyses I carried out elsewhere;[7] a few basic points will suffice. When labour performs overseeing and coordination tasks, that is, when it 'steps to the *side* of the production process instead of being its chief actor',[8] its duties no longer amount to the accomplishment of a single particular objective, but to modulating (and varying, and intensifying) social *cooperation*, that is, that set of systemic relations and connections that constitutes by now the actual 'foundation-stone of production and of wealth'.[9] Such a modulation takes place by means of linguistic tasks that, far from giving rise to a final product, are exhausted within the communicative interaction determined by their own implementation.

Post-Fordist activity presupposes and, at the same time, incessantly re-elaborates the 'publicly organized space' (the space of cooperation, indeed) of which Arendt speaks as the indispensable prerequisite of both the dancer and the politician. The 'presence of others' is both an instrument and an object of labour; therefore, productive procedures always require a certain degree of virtuosity—they imply actual *political actions*.[10] Mass intellectuality

---

7 Paolo Virno, *Convention and Materialism: Uniqueness without Aura* (Cambridge, MA: MIT Press, 2021).

8 Marx, *Grundrisse*, Notebook 7. (emphasis added).

9 Marx, *Grundrisse*, Notebook 7.

10 In his novel *It's a Hard Life* (New York: The Viking Press, 1965 [1962]), Luciano Bianciardi offers a grotesque and perspicuous portrayal of labour in the cultural industry at the end of the 1950s. Let us read a passage on the vicissitudes of those who are devoted to an activity that does not create any

lasting work. 'I was given the sack for the same reason, because I dragged my feet, moved slowly, and kept looking all around when there was no actual need to. In our business you have to lift your feet smartly, plant them down again solidly, move briskly and raise the dust, if possible a cloud of it to hide behind. It's quite different from being a peasant or worker. A peasant moves slowly, because his work depends so much on the seasons, he cannot sow in July and reap in February. A worker moves quickly, but only because he is on the assembly line, because his tempo of production has been calculated, and if he does not keep it up there will be trouble [. . .]. But the fact of the matter is that the peasant's is a primary job and the worker's a secondary one. The former produces something out of nothing, and the latter turns things into something else. In both cases it is easy to apply a yardstick, a quantitative one, the productivity of the factory or the profitability of the farm. But in businesses of our kind there is no quantitative yardstick. How can you calculate the value of the work done by a priest, an advertising man, a public relations officer? *They neither produce something out of nothing nor turn one thing into another.* Their jobs are neither primary nor secondary. In fact they are tertiary or [. . .] I should call them quaternary. They are not instruments of production, or even conveyor belts. At best they are lubricants, or so much vaseline. How can one assess the value of a priest, advertising man or public relations officer, or calculate the amount of faith, acquisitiveness or good will that they succeed in stimulating? The only measuring rod that can be applied to them is the ability of each to remain afloat and rise higher, to become bishops, in fact. In other words, those who choose a tertiary or quaternary calling require *gifts and attitudes of the political type*. Politics, as everyone knows, has longed ceased to be the science of good government and has become the art of the acquisition and preservation of power. A politician's merit is not gauged by the good he does, but by the speed with which he reaches the top and the time he is able to maintain himself there. [. . .] In the tertiary and quaternary occupations, *as there is no visible production of goods to serve as a yardstick*, the criterion is the same' (pp. 104–6; emphasis added). In this passage, there is a formidable intuition. Bianciardi observes that the new and extravagant professions linked to communication do not give rise to a tangible product, that is, they do not imply a defined outcome as commodities. And he adds that they (a rather clumsy term that has been used to specify a quality of post-Fordist labour-power in its *entirety*, rather than a group of specific jobs) is required to exercise the art of the possible, deal with the unexpected, and benefit from an opportunity. When the motto of labour producing surplus value sarcastically becomes 'politics first!', politics in the strict sense of the word is dismissed and paralysed.

For that matter, what does the capitalist slogan of 'total quality' mean if not the request to put to work everything that traditionally lies outside work, in other words, communicative skills and a taste for Action? And how can the whole experience of an individual be included in the process of production if not by obliging him to carry out a sequence of variations on the theme, performances, and improvisations? In a parody of self-realization, such a sequence actually marks the epitome of subjection. Nobody is so poor as those who

---

require 'gifts and attitudes of the political type'. What is decisive here is the logical nexus, and even the authentic causal relation, between the two aspects: precisely because it lacks a 'work' endowed with an autonomous life (which can therefore be valued in quantitative terms), work behaviour resembles public praxis and Action. When one does not produce new objects, but sets up communicative networks, the reign of politics begins. In Bianciardi's novel, there are certainly some outmoded references. The 'tertiary and quaternary' jobs are still perceived as something unnatural and parasitic, which can only loosely be called 'labour'. The cultural industry is considered as a clownish exception with regard to the rules, which are nonetheless dictated by the traditional factory. Moreover, the idea of politics evoked by the novelist is very superficial—jostling, abuse of power, and blind thirst for it. However, the fact remains that, for Bianciardi, the political character of labour hinges on the absence of 'work'. And this is a great intuition, whose value is strengthened when the bygone exception becomes the new rule, namely, when the symbiosis between labour and communication amounts to a pervasive trait of the entire process of production (including 'primary' and 'secondary' labour, to put it with Bianciardi).

see their relation with the 'presence of others', that is, their having-language, reduced to wage labour.[11]

---

11 It is worth asking what relationship exists between the peculiar characters of cultural industry (of which, among others, Bianciardi speaks in It's a Hard Life) and post-Fordism in general. It is well known that, starting with Adorno and Horkheimer, the 'factories of the soul' have meticulously been scrutinized by critics, who searched for all that made them similar to assembly lines. The crucial point was showing how capitalism was able to mechanize and divide spiritual production precisely in the same way as it had mechanized and divided agriculture or metalworking. Seriality, insignificance of individual duties, and the econometry of emotions and feelings—these are the usual refrains. Certainly, it was admitted that some aspects of what we could define as 'the production of communication by means of communication' were resistant to a complete assimilation into the Fordist organization of the work process. But they were rightly considered as irrelevant residues, modest disturbances, and minor waste products. Yet, assessing things retrospectively, it is not difficult to recognize that these 'residues' were instead loaded with future—they were not echoes of a previous age but actual *omens*. In short, the informality of communicative action, the competitive interaction typical of an editorial board, the flash of unexpectedness that can flare up a television programme, and, generally, everything that would be *anti-functional* to tighten and regulate beyond a certain threshold within cultural industry, has now become, in the post-Fordist age, the central and propulsive kernel of social production as a whole. In this sense, it is not exaggerated to argue that 'Toyotism' amounts, at least in part, to the application of operational modules that were once inherent only to the cultural industry to factories that produce lasting goods. The sociological continuation of It's a Hard Life may perhaps be found in the inquiries into working behaviour at the Melfi FIAT factory.

3.

Public Intellect: The Virtuosos' Score

What is the score that post-Fordist workers have continuously performed from the moment they were led to demonstrate their virtuosity? The basic answer goes as follows: the sui generis score of contemporary labour is the Intellect as public Intellect, or general intellect, that is, an overarching social knowledge and a common linguistic competence. We could also say that production requires virtuosity, and hence introjects several particular traits of political action, precisely and only because the Intellect has become the main force of production, the premise and epicentre of every *poiesis*.

Hannah Arendt impulsively rejects the very idea of a *public intellect*. In her view, reflection, thought, and mental life in general do not share anything with the care of common affairs that, on the contrary, involves 'exposing oneself to others'. Marx does instead hint at the intrusion of the Intellect in the world of appearances, first in his concept of 'real abstraction', and then especially in that of 'general intellect'. While real abstraction is an empirical fact (for instance, the exchange of equivalents) that has the subtle structure of a pure thought, the general intellect rather marks the stage at which pure thoughts as such have the value and the typical bearing of facts (if you like, this is the stage at which mental abstractions are as such immediately real abstractions).

However, Marx conceives the general intellect as a 'scientific capacity' objectivized in the system of machines, and thus as fixed capital. In this way, he reduces the conspicuousness and public character of the Intellect to the technological application of natural sciences to the process of production. The crucial step amounts instead to acknowledging that the general intellect is presented today as the direct attribute of living labour, the repertoire of a diffuse intelligentsia, and the score that combines a multitude. Moreover, the analysis of post-Fordist production compels us to take this step. In fact, a decisive role is played here by conceptual constellations and thought patterns that can never be contained within fixed capital, since they are inseparable from the interaction of a plurality of living subjects. Obviously, what is at stake is not the scientific erudition of the individual worker. What comes to the fore, acquiring the rank of public resource, are only (but this 'only' means everything) the most generic aptitudes of the mind—the faculty of language, the inclination to learn, the capacity to abstract and correlate, the access to self-reflection.

Literally, we should understand 'general intellect' as *intellect in general*. Now, it goes without saying that the Intellect-in-general amounts to a 'score' only in a broad sense. We are certainly not dealing with a specific musical composition (such as Bach's *Goldberg Variations*) performed by an unsurpassed pianist (such as Glenn Gould), but, indeed, with a mere *faculty*—or better, the faculty that makes every composition (and experience) possible. In this case, the virtuosic performance that never gives rise to a work cannot even presuppose it. Instead it amounts to making the Intellect resonate *as* an aptitude. Its only 'score' is the condition of possibility of all scores. This virtuosity is not an unusual fact, nor does it require some rare talent. Suffice it to think of the expertise with which every speaking being draws from the inexhaustible potentiality of language (as the opposite of a defined 'work') in order to utter a contingent and unrepeatable statement.

3.1

The Intellect becomes public when it is combined with Labour; however, as soon as it is combined with it, its typical public character is at the same time inhibited and distorted. Evoked always anew as a productive force, the public character is suppressed ever anew as an actual *public sphere*, possible source of political Action, and different constitutional principle.

The general intellect is the foundation of a social cooperation that is broader than the one specifically dependent on labour—broader and, at the same time, completely heterogeneous. While the connections of the productive process are based on the technical *division* of tasks, the concerted action hinging on the general intellect moves from the common participation in mental life, or, in other words, from the preliminary *sharing* of communicative and cognitive aptitudes. However, rather than eliminating the compulsions of capitalist production, the *surplus* cooperation of the Intellect figures as capitalism's most eminent resource. Its heterogeneity has neither voice nor visibility. Actually, insofar as the conspicuousness of the Intellect becomes an aspect of Labour, the acting in concert outside of labour caused by surplus cooperation is in turn subjected to the criteria and restrictions that characterize the factory regime.

This paradoxical situation has two main consequences. The first concerns the nature and form of political power. The peculiar public character of the Intellect, deprived of its proper expression by a Labour that nonetheless lays claim to it as a productive force, is indirectly manifested in the sphere of the State through the *hypertrophic growth of administrative apparatuses*. The kernel of statehood is no longer the politico-parliamentarian system but the Administration; and this is indeed the case because Administration consists of an authoritarian concretion of the general intellect, the merging point between knowledge and command, and the reversed image of surplus cooperation. Admittedly, the growing and determining weight of bureaucracy in the 'body politic'—the predominance of administrative orders over law—has been observed for decades; but here I would like to point at an unprecedented threshold. In short, we no longer face the well-known processes of State rationalization, but, on the contrary, it is by now necessary to acknowledge the accomplishment of the *statization of the Intellect*. The age-old expression 'raison d'état' acquires for the first time a non-metaphorical meaning. If Hobbes and the other great theoreticians of 'political unity' saw the principle of legitimation of absolute power in the *transfer* of the natural right of each individual to the person of the sovereign, today we should instead speak of the *transfer* of the Intellect—or better, its immediate and irreducible public character—to state Administration.

The second consequence concerns the actual nature of the post-Fordist regime. Given that the 'publicly organized space' opened by the Intellect is repeatedly reduced to labour cooperation—a dense network of hierarchical relations—the decisive function of the 'presence of others' in every concrete productive operation takes the form of *personal dependence*. In other words, virtuosic activity appears as universal *servile labour*. The affinity between the pianist and the waiter that Marx glimpsed finds an unexpected confirmation in the age in which all wage labour has some traits of the performing artist. When 'the product is not separable from the act of producing', this act calls into question the person who carries it out, and especially the relationship between this person and the one who has ordered it or to whom it is addressed. On the one hand, the putting into work of what is *common*—the Intellect and Language—refutes the impersonal technical division of tasks; on the other, to the extent that such a commonality is not translated into a public sphere—a political community—it brings about a viscous personalization of subjection.

4.
Exodus

The cornerstone of political action (or better, the step to be taken and that alone can save it from the current paralysis) consists in developing the public character of the Intellect outside of Labour, and in opposition to it. This issue has two distinct aspects, which are nevertheless strictly complimentary. On the one hand, the general intellect affirms itself as an autonomous public sphere, and thus avoids 'transferring' its potency to the absolute power of Administration, only if it cuts the link that binds it to the production of commodities and wage labour. On the other hand, the subversion of the capitalist relations of production can by now manifest itself only with the establishment of a non-state public sphere—a political community that hinges on the general intellect. The salient traits of post-Fordist experience—servile virtuosity, valorization of the very faculty of language, inevitable relation with the 'presence of others', etc.—postulate as a conflictual retaliation nothing less than a radically new form of democracy.

I call Exodus the mass defection from the State, the alliance between general intellect and political Action, and the transit towards the public sphere of the Intellect. Thus, the term does not at all point at a miserable existential strategy, exiting on tiptoes from the back-door, or searching for a sheltering hole. On the contrary, what I mean by 'exodus' is a model for thorough action, one that is capable of confronting the 'ultimate things' of modern politics—the great themes articulated in turn by Hobbes, Rousseau, Lenin and Schmitt (I am thinking here of crucial couples such as command/obedience, public/private, friend/enemy, consensus/violence, etc.). Not unlike what happened in the seventeenth century under the pressure of the civil wars of religion, today we need to delimit anew the *field of common affairs*. This delimitation must exhibit the opportunity for freedom inherent to the unprecedented interweaving of Labour, Action, and Intellect, which, instead, we have so far only suffered.

4.1

Exodus is the foundation of a Republic. But the very idea of 'republic' requires the dismissal of the state system. The political action of exodus therefore consists of a *resourceful withdrawal*. Only those who open a way out are able to found something; but, vice versa, only those who found something manage to find the crossing that will enable them to leave Egypt. In the remaining part of these notes, I intend to describe in detail the theme of Exodus, that is, the theme of Action as a resourceful withdrawal (or foundational dismissal) by means of a series of keywords, the most important of which are: Disobedience, Intemperance, Multitude, Soviet, Example, Right of Resistance and Miracle.

5.

The Virtue of Intemperance

Today, 'civil disobedience' stands for the basic and unavoidable form of political action—but only if we emancipate it from the liberal tradition in which it has been trapped. It is not a matter of disregarding a specific law because it is incoherent or in contradiction with other fundamental norms, such as the provisions of the constitution; in fact, in this case insubordination would only witness to a more profound loyalty to state command. On the contrary, however domesticated its individual manifestations might be, the radical Disobedience I am interested in must call into question the State's very faculty of command.

According to Hobbes, with the establishment of the 'body politic' we oblige ourselves to obey even *before* we know what will be ordered: 'Our obligation to civil obedience, by vertue whereof the civill Lawes are valid, is before all civill Law.'[1] For this reason, there is no particular law that explicitly enjoins us not to rebel. If the unconditional acceptance of command were not already *presupposed*, concrete legislative dispositions (including, obviously, the one that says 'thou shalt not rebel') would have no validity. Hobbes argues

---

1 Thomas Hobbes, *De Cive* (Oxford: Oxford University Press, 1983), p. 181.

that the original bond of obedience derives from 'natural law', that is, the common interest in self-preservation and safety. And yet he hastens to add that 'natural' law—the Superlaw that imposes obedience to all the orders of the sovereign—really becomes a law only when one overcomes the state of nature, and hence when the State is already established. A real paradox emerges here; the obligation to obedience is both cause and effect of the existence of the State; it is supported by something of which it is nonetheless the foundation. At the same time, it precedes and follows the formation of 'supreme power'.

Political Action targets the preliminary obedience without content on the basis of which alone the melancholic dialectic of acquiescence and transgression can then be developed. By violating a specific directive concerning the dismantling of the healthcare system or the interruption of immigration, we go back to the concealed presupposition of every imperative directive and threaten its implementation. Radical Disobedience is itself 'before all civil Law', since it does not limit itself to violating civil laws, but calls into question the very foundation of their validity.

5.1

In order to justify the pre-emptive obligation to compliance, an end-of-the-millennium Hobbes should appeal to the technical rationality of the production process—the general intellect as the despotic organization of wage Labour—rather than to a 'natural law'. Like 'natural law', the 'law of general intellect' has a paradoxical structure: on the one hand, it seems to found the command of state Administration demanding the respect for every decision it may take; on the other, it presents itself as an actual *law* only because (and after) the Administration already exercises an unconditional command.

Radical Disobedience breaks this virtuous circle according to which the public Intellect figures, at the same time, as premise and consequence of the State. It breaks this circle thanks to the double movement I hinted at earlier. First of all, radical Disobedience highlights and positively develops the aspects of the general intellect that clash with the further maintenance of wage Labour. On this basis, it enforces the practical potency of the Intellect against the decisional faculty of the Administration. Freed from the production of surplus value, the Intellect is no longer a 'natural law' of late capitalism, but the matrix of a non-state Republic.

5.2

Disobedience is nourished by social conflicts that manifest themselves not only and not so much as protest but especially as defection—in Albert O. Hirschman's words, not as 'voice' but as 'exit'.[2]

Nothing is less passive than flight. The 'exit' modifies the conditions within which the confrontation takes place, instead of presupposing them as an unmovable horizon—it changes the context in which the problem arose, instead of tackling the problem by choosing one or the other expected alternative. In short, the 'exit' consists in an audacious invention that alters the rules of the game and makes our adversary lose his bearings. Suffice it to think of the mass flight from the factory regime enacted by US workers in the middle of the nineteenth century: heading off to the 'frontier' to colonize low-cost lands, they seized the truly extraordinary opportunity of making their own initial condition *reversible*.[3]

---

2 Albert O. Hirschman, *Exit, Voice and Loyalty* (Cambridge, MA: Harvard University Press, 1970).

3 Marx analyses the economical and political role of the North American 'frontier' in the last chapter of the first book of *Capital*, entitled 'The Modern Theory of Colonization'. Marx writes: 'There, the absolute numbers of the population increase much more quickly than in the mother country, because many workers enter the colonial world as ready-made adults, and still the labour-market is always understocked. The law of the

Something similar happened in Italy at the end of the 1970s, when the young workforce, contradicting all expectations, preferred precariousness and part-time work over permanent jobs in large companies. Albeit only for a short time, occupational mobility functioned as a political resource, causing the eclipse of industrial discipline and permitting a certain degree of self-determination. Even in this case pre-established roles were deserted and a 'territory' unknown to official maps was colonized.

Defection is the opposite of the desperate 'You have nothing to lose but your own chains'; instead, it hinges on a latent richness, an exuberance of possibilities, and ultimately the principle of the *tertium datur*. But, in the post-Fordist age, what is the virtual abundance that elicits the option of flight to the detriment of the option of resistance? Evidently, what is at stake is not a spatial frontier, but an excess of knowledge, communication, and acting in concert implied by the public character of the general intellect. The act of collective imagination I call 'defection' gives an autonomous, affirmative, and highlighted expression to this excess, thus preventing its 'transfer' into the power of state Administration.

---

supply and demand of labour collapses completely. On the one hand, the old world constantly throws in capital, thirsting after exploitation and "abstinence"; on the other, the regular reproduction of the wage-labourer as a wage-labourer comes up against the most mischievous obstacles, which are in part insuperable. And what becomes of the production of redundant wage-labourers, redundant, that is, in proportion to the accumulation of capital? Today's wage-labourer is tomorrow's independent peasant or artisan, working for himself. He vanishes from the labour-market—but not into the workhouse. This constant transformation of wage-labourers into independent producers, who work for themselves instead of for capital, and enrich themselves instead of the capitalist gentlemen, reacts in its turn very adversely on the conditions of the labour-market. Not only does the degree of exploitation of the wage-labourer remain indecently low. The wage-labourer also loses, along with the relation of dependence, the feeling of dependence on the abstemious capitalist' (Marx, *Capital*, VOL. 1, pp. 935–6).

Radical Disobedience therefore involves a set of *positive actions*. It is not a resentful omission but an undertaken omission. Besides, the sovereign order is not carried out because one is too busy with setting up differently the question that it claims to settle.

5.3

It is worth recalling the distinction between intemperance (*akrasia*) and incontinence (*akolasia*)—which was very clear in ancient ethics but subsequently almost always overlooked. While incontinence amounts to vulgar unruliness, disregard for the laws, and giving in to the most immediate whims, Intemperance consists instead of opposing intellectual knowledge to ethical and political norms. We adopt a theoretical premise in place of a practical one as a guiding principle of action, and the consequences that follow may be extravagant and dangerous with regard to the harmony of social life. According to Aristotle,[4] the intemperate person is depraved, because he juxtaposes and confuses two kinds of essentially different discourses. He does not ignore the law, nor is satisfied with contesting it, but dismisses it in the most serious manner since he derives his public conduct from that pure Intellect which, having its own sphere, should not interfere with the events of the *polis*.

Exodus finds in Intemperance its main virtue. The preliminary obligation to obedience to the State is not disregarded out of incontinence but in the name of a systematic combination of Intellect and political Action. Every constructive defection relies on the conspicuous reality of the general intellect, and draws from it practical consequences that are at odds with 'civil laws'. In the intemperate reference to the Intellect-in-general a *non-servile virtuosity* is finally outlined.

---

4 Aristotle, *Nicomachean Ethics* 1147a25–b20.

6.

In Praise of the Multitude

The decisive political contrast is that which opposes the Multitude to the People. According to Hobbes (but also a good part of the democratic-socialist tradition) the notion of the people is strictly linked with the existence of the State, and is even one of its reverberations: 'The People is somewhat that is *one*, having *one* will, and to whom *one* action may be attributed. [. . .] The People rules in all governments' and, reciprocally, 'the King is the People.'[1] The progressivist refrain about 'popular sovereignty' has as its acrid counterpoint the identification of the people with the sovereign, or, if you prefer, the *popularity of the king*. On the other hand, the Multitude avoids political unity, is recalcitrant to obedience, and never attains the status of a juridical person; consequently, it cannot 'promise, contract, acquire Right, [and] conveigh Right'.[2] It is anti-state, but, precisely for this reason, also anti-popular; when citizens rebel against the State, they are 'the Multitude against the People'.[3]

---

[1] Hobbes, *De Cive*, p. 151.

[2] Hobbes, *De Cive*, p. 92.

[3] Hobbes, *De Cive*, p. 152.

For the seventeenth-century apologists of sovereign power, 'multitude' was a radically negative limit-concept—a resurgence of the state of nature within civil society; a resilient yet shapeless remainder; a metaphor of a possible crisis. Later on, liberal thought domesticated the anxiety caused by the 'many' by means of the public/private dichotomy. The Multitude is private in the literal sense of the term—*deprived* of a face and voice—as well as in its juridical sense—alien to the sphere of common affairs. In its turn, democratic-socialist theory brandished the couple collective/individual: while the collectivity of producers (as the ultimate embodiment of the People) identifies with the State—be it Scalfaro's or Ceausescu's State[4]—the Multitude is confined within individual experience, and thus condemned to impotence.

This destiny of marginality has now come to an end. Instead of amounting to a natural prequel, the Multitude presents itself as a *historical result* and a mature arrival point of the transformations that have taken place in the process of production and the forms of life. The Many burst on the scene, and stay there as absolute protagonists, as soon as the crisis of the society of Labour is being played out. Abrogating the border between productive and personal time, as well as the difference between professional skills and political aptitudes, post-Fordist social cooperation creates a new species for which the dichotomies public/private and collective/individual sound farcical. Being neither 'producers' nor 'citizens', modern virtuosos ultimately attain the rank of Multitude.

We are dealing with a lasting outcome, not a tumultuous intermezzo. In fact, the new Multitude is not a whirlpool of atoms that *still* lacks unity, but the form of political existence that is being affirmed *starting from* a One—the public Intellect—radically heterogeneous to the State. The Many do not make pacts, or transfer their rights to the sovereign, because they already possess a common

---

4 Oscar Luigi Scalfaro was the President of Italy from 1992 to 1999 [Trans.].

'score'; they never converge into a *volonté générale* because they already share a general intellect.

6.1

The Multitude obstructs and unsettles the mechanisms of political representation. It expresses itself as an ensemble of 'acting minorities', none of which, however, aspires to be transformed into a majority. It develops a *power* that is resistant to becoming a *government*.

The fact is that each of the Many remains inseparable from the 'presence of others', and unconceivable outside of the linguistic cooperation—or acting-in-concert—entailed by this presence. But cooperation—unlike individual labour time or the individual right of citizenship—is not a 'substance' that can be extrapolated and commuted. Certainly, it can be subjugated, but not represented, let alone delegated. The Multitude, which has its own exclusive way of being in acting-in-concert, is infiltrated by all sorts of kapos and many quislings, but it does not validate any stand-ins or nominees.

By now the States of the developed West conform themselves to the political non-representability of the post-Fordist workforce; they even gain strength from it, deriving from it a paradoxical legitimation for their authoritarian restructuring. The mature and irreversible crisis of representation gives them an opportunity to liquidate every remaining semblance of public sphere, to expand beyond measure—as seen—the prerogatives of Administration to the detriment of the political-parliamentarian field, and to turn the state of emergency into something usual. Institutional reforms create rules and procedures that are necessary to govern a Multitude to which one can no longer superimpose the reassuring physiognomy of the People.

As interpreted by the post-Keynesian State, the structural weakening of representative democracy is manifested as an increasing restriction of democracy tout-court. However, it goes without saying that, if it is carried out in the name of the values of representation, the opposition to this involution is useless and pathetic—as ineffective as preaching chastity to sparrows. Today, democratic force coincides with the experimentation of forms of *non-representative and extra-parliamentarian democracy.* Everything else is petulant chitchat.

6.2

The democracy of the Multitude takes seriously the diagnosis Carl Schmitt proposed, somewhat bitterly, in the last years of his life: 'The age of the state is now coming to an end [. . .]. The State as a model of political unity and as the bearer of the most extraordinary of all monopolies—the monopoly on political decision-making—is about to be dethroned.'[5] But it also makes an important specification; the monopoly on decision-making is truly taken away from the State only if it ceases to be a monopoly once and for all. The public sphere of the Intellect, that is, the Republic of the Many, is a *centrifugal force;* in other words, it rules out not only the permanence but also the reconstitution of any form of unitary 'body politic'. In order to make the anti-monopolistic drive last, the Republican conspiracy is embodied in those democratic organizations that, being non-representative, prevent any reconfiguration of 'political unity'.

It is well known that Hobbes scorned 'irregular political systemes', whose uncanny characteristic is that they foreshadow the Multitude within the People: 'Leagues, or sometimes meer concourse of people, without union to any particular designe, [or] obligation of one to another'.[6] Well, the Republic of the Many precisely consists of institutions of this kind: *leagues, councils,* and *soviets.* But, contrary to Hobbes's malevolent assessment, these are certainly not ephemeral gatherings whose unfolding leaves the rituals of sovereignty undisturbed. Leagues, councils, and soviets—the organs

---

5 Schmitt, *Der Begriff des Politischen,* p. 10.
6 Hobbes, *Leviathan,* p. 163.

of non-representative democracy—give instead political expression to the acting-in-concert that—being organized by the general intellect—always already enjoy a *public* character which is fundamentally different from the one assembled in the sovereign. The public sphere delineated by the 'concourses' in which there is no 'obligation of one to another' determines the *king's solitude*, that is, it reduces the state complex to a very private—overbearing yet marginal—*inner-city gang*.

The soviets of the Multitude interfere in a conflictual way with the State's administrative apparatuses, with a view to eroding its prerogatives and absorb its responsibilities. They translate into a republican praxis—the care of common affairs—the same basic resources—knowledge, communication, relationship with the 'presence of others'—that hold the stage in post-Fordist production. They emancipate *virtuosistic cooperation* from its present combination with wage Labour, showing with positive actions how the one exceeds and contradicts the other.

In opposition to representation and delegation, the soviets propose an operative style that is far more complex, and centred on the *Example* and *political reproducibility*. I call 'exemplary' the practical initiative that has the authority of the *prototype,* exhibiting in a particular case the possible alliance between general intellect and Republic, and not the normativity of command. Whether it is a question of income distribution or the organization of schools, the functioning of the media or urban planning, the soviets elaborate paradigmatic actions that are capable of sparking a new combination of knowledge, ethical propensities, techniques, and desires. The Example is not the empirical application of a universal concept; it rather has the singularity and qualitative accomplishment that, speaking about mental life, we normally attribute to an *idea*. All in all, it is a species that consists of only one individual. For this reason, the Example can be reproduced politically, but never transposed into an omnivorous 'general programme'.

7.
The Right to Resistance

The atrophy of political Action has had as its corollary the conviction that there is no longer any enemy, but only incoherent interlocutors, trapped in equivocation and as yet not enlightened. The abandonment of the notion of enmity, deemed to be too harsh or improper, betrays a considerable optimism. In other words, one thinks oneself to be 'swimming with the current'[1] (this is how Walter Benjamin reprimanded German social-democracy in the 1930s). It does not really matter if the benign 'current' assumes different names at each turn—progress; the development of productive forces; the individuation of a form of life that avoids inauthenticity; the general intellect. Naturally, one takes into consideration the possibility of not being at all able to 'swim', that is, of not knowing how to define in clear terms what the politics appropriate to our times consists of. However, this caution does not elide but instead corroborates a fundamental persuasion: as long as one learns to 'swim', and hence to the extent that one thinks possible freedom correctly, the 'current' will irresistibly lead one forward. Thus one does not take into account the interdiction that institutions, interests, and material forces oppose to

---

1 Walter Benjamin, 'Theses on the Philosophy of History' in *Illuminations* (New York: Schocken, 1968), p. 258.

the shrewd swimmer; one ignores the catastrophe that often befalls precisely and only the person who has seen things correctly. But there is worse: the one who does not care about defining the specific nature of the *enemy*, and individuating the places in which his power is embedded and the bounds he imposes are stricter, cannot even indicate the positive instance for which to fight—the alternative way of being that is worth hoping for.

The theory of Exodus gives back to the concept of enmity all its significance, but it stresses the peculiar traits it assumes when 'the age of the state is coming to an end'. How is the relationship friend/enemy manifested for the post-Fordist Multitude, which, although it certainly tends to dismantle 'supreme power', is also definitely not amenable to turning itself into a State?

7.1

In the first place, we need to acknowledge a change in the *geometry of hostility*. The enemy no longer figures as a parallel straight line, or a specular interface, that opposes point by point the trenches and bunkers occupied by friends, but rather as a segment that repeatedly intersects a sinusoidal line of flight. And this happens especially because friends are evacuating predictable positions, giving rise to a sequence of *constructive defections*. In military terms, the contemporary enemy continues to imitate the Pharaoh's army; it chases the fugitives, massacring their rear guard, but never manages to get ahead of them and confront them. Now, the very fact that hostility has become *asymmetrical* compels us to grant an autonomous significance to the concept of friendship, releasing it from the subaltern and parasitic status Carl Schmitt assigned it. Far from being characterized only by his sharing our same enemy, the friend is defined by the relations of solidarity that are established during the flight, by the necessity of inventing *together* opportunities that have not been computed up until that point, and by our common participation in the Republic. Friendship is always more extensive than the front along which the Pharaoh unleashes his incursions. But this overabundance does not at all involve a sophisticated indifference towards what happens on the line of fire. On the contrary, the asymmetry makes it possible to ambush the enemy, confusing and blinding those we want to leave behind.

Secondly, it is necessary to carefully specify what is, today, the *gradation of hostility*. By way of contrast, it is useful to recall Schmitt's proverbial distinction between *relative* and *absolute* enmity.[2] The European wars among states in the eighteenth century were circumscribed and regulated by criteria for conflicts; in them each contender recognized the other as the legitimate bearer of sovereignty, and thus as a subject endowed with equal prerogatives. According to Schmitt, these were happy times, which are irrevocably over. In our century, the proletarian revolutions have uncompromisingly disinhibited hostility, elevating civil war to the implicit model of every conflict. When what is at stake is state power, that is, sovereignty, enmity becomes absolute. But is Schmitt's parameter still reliable? We should be doubtful, since it ignores the telluric movement that is truly decisive—namely, a kind of hostility that does not aspire to transfer the monopoly of political decision-making into new hands, but rather demands its abrogation.

The model of absolute enmity falls apart, not because it is extremist or violent, but, paradoxically, because it is not radical enough. In fact, the republican Multitude aims at destroying what amounts to the victor's coveted prize in this model. Civil war perfectly suits only ethnic feuds, in which what is decided is still *who* the sovereign is, while it turns out to be totally incongruous to conflicts that, undermining the economical-juridical order of the capitalist State, call into question sovereignty as such. The different 'acting minorities' multiply the non-state centres of political

---

2 Carl Schmitt, *Theory of the Partisan* (New York: Telos Press, 2007).

decision-making, without having to propose the formation of a new *volonté générale* (and actually dismissing its foundation). This entails the stable prevalence of an intermediate state between war and peace. On the one hand, the battle to secure 'the most extraordinary of all monopolies' does not presuppose any conclusion different from total victory or total defeat; on the other, the instance of utmost radicalism—which is *anti-monopolistic*—alternates instead between breaking off relations and negotiation, between the intransigence that does not rule out any means and the compromises necessary to carve out free zones and neutral fields. Being neither relative in the sense of the *jus publicum europaeum* that used to moderate the contests between sovereign States, nor absolute in the manner of civil wars, the enmity of the Multitude may perhaps be seen as *unlimitedly reactive*.

7.2

Far from suggesting a defenceless meekness, the new geometry and gradation of hostility demands a meticulous redefinition of the role carried out by violence in political Action. Since Exodus is a resourceful withdrawal, the use of force is no longer to be adapted to the conquest of state power in the land of the Pharaoh, but to the safeguarding of the forms of life and the communitarian relationships experienced along the way. The works of friendship are worth defending at all costs. Violence is not longing for 'the morrows that sing', but ensures respect for and persistence with what was sketched yesterday. It does not innovate but continues something that already exists: autonomous expressions of the acting-in-concert hinging on the general intellect; organizations of non-representative democracy; forms of assistance and reciprocal protection (in short, of welfare) originating outside and against State Administration. We are thus dealing with a *conservational violence*.

The pre-modern political category of *jus resistentiae*, the Right to Resistance, can well be applied to the extreme conflicts of the post-Fordist metropolis. In medieval jurisprudence, this phrase did not refer at all to the obvious faculty to defend oneself when attacked, nor to a general uprising against constituted power. There is a clear distinction between resistance, on the one hand, and *seditio* and *rebellio*, on the other. The Right to Resistance has a very specific and subtle meaning. It authorizes the use of violence whenever a craft-guild, or the entire community, or even individual citizens, see some of their *positive prerogatives*—actually acquired or traditionally valid—altered by the central power. The crucial point is therefore the preservation of a transformation that took place in the past, and the sanctioning of a common way of being that already stands out. Strictly correlated to radical Disobedience and the virtue of Intemperance, the *jus resistentiae* appears today to be the ultimate and most updated motto in terms of 'legality' and 'illegality'. While the foundation of the Republic rejects the prospect of civil war, it nonetheless postulates a meticulous Right to Resistance.

8.

The Expected Unforeseen

Labour, Action, Intellect; along the lines of a tradition that dates back to Aristotle and was still 'common sense' for the generation that entered politics in the 1960s, Hannah Arendt irrevocably separates these three spheres of human experience, showing their reciprocal incommensurability. Although they are adjacent and even superimposed, these different fields remain unrelated. Actually, they exclude one another; when we make politics, we do not produce, nor are we absorbed in intellectual contemplation. When we work, we do not act politically by exposing ourselves to the presence of others, nor are we participating in mental life. Those who devote themselves to pure reflection are temporarily withdrawn from the world of appearances, and therefore do not act or produce. The message of Arendt's *The Human Condition* seems to be 'to each his own and every man for himself'. Consequently, when she argues with admirable passion for the specific value of political Action, fighting against its contraction in mass society, Arendt presupposes that the two other fundamental spheres—Labour and Intellect—have remained unaltered with regard to their qualitative structure. Of course, Labour has been extended beyond measure; of course, thought is weak and paralysed; however, the former is still an organic exchange with nature, a social metabolism, and a production of new objects, and the latter is still a solitary activity, in itself alien to the care of common affairs.

It should be clear by now that my argument is radically opposed to the conceptual framework proposed by Arendt and the tradition by which it is inspired. Let us summarize what I have said so far. The decline of Action depends on the qualitative modifications that took place both in the sphere of Labour and in that of the Intellect, whereby a strong intimacy has been established between them. Connected with Labour, the Intellect (as an aptitude or *faculty*, and certainly not as the receptacle of specialized knowledge) becomes *public*, conspicuous, and mundane; in other words, its nature as a shared resource and common good comes to the fore. Reciprocally, when the potency of the general intellect amounts to the principle pillar of social production, Labour looks like an activity-without-work, resembling in every respect to the *virtuosistic performances* that are based on a clear relation with the 'presence of others'. But is virtuosity not the characteristic trait of political action? We therefore need to conclude that post-Fordist production has incorporated the typical modalities of Action, and, by doing so, eclipsed it. This metamorphosis is by no means emancipatory; under the auspices of wage Labour, the virtuosistic relationship with the 'presence of others' is translated into *personal dependence*; although it closely recalls political praxis, activity-without-work is reduced to a very modern form of *servile service*.

In the second part of this essay, I claimed that political Action is redeemed when it joins forces with the public Intellect (when this Intellect is freed from wage Labour—and even outlines its critique with the tact of a corrosive acid). Ultimately, Action consists in articulating the general intellect as a non-state public sphere, field of common affairs, and Republic. The Exodus—during which the new alliance between Intellect and Action is realized—has some fixed stars in its heaven: radical Disobedience, Intemperance, Multitude, Soviet,

Example, Right to Resistance. These categories allude to a coming political theory capable of facing the crisis of the twentieth-century old regime, by envisioning a solution that is radically anti-Hobbesian.

8.1

Arendt claims that political Action is a new beginning that interrupts and contradicts consolidated automatic processes.[1] Action has thus something of the *miracle*, since it is itself unexpected and surprising. Now, to conclude, it is worth asking whether the theme of Miracle might be relevant to the theory of Exodus—which is otherwise irreconcilable with Arendt's position.

This is indeed a recurrent theme in great political thinking, especially of the reactionary kind. For Hobbes, it is the sovereign who decides which events deserve the rank of miracles, that is, transcend ordinary laws.[2] Conversely, miracles stop as soon as the sovereign forbids them. It is well known that Schmitt adopts a similar stance when he identifies the core of political power with the discretion to proclaim the state of exception that suspends the constitutional order: 'The exception in jurisprudence is analogous to the miracle in theology.'[3] Spinoza's democratic radicalism instead refutes the theological-political value of miraculous exception. However, there is an ambivalent aspect in his reasoning. In fact, according to Spinoza, unlike the universal laws of nature with which God is identified, the miracle expresses only a 'limited power', that is, it is something specifically human; rather than consolidating faith, it actually makes us 'doubt God and everything',[4] paving the way for atheism. But are

---

1 Arendt, 'What is Freedom?', pp. 459–60.

2 Hobbes, *Leviathan*, chapter 37.

3 Carl Schmitt, *Political Theology: Four Chapters on the Concept of Sovereignty* (Cambridge, MA: MIT Press, 1985), p. 36.

4 Baruch Spinoza, 'Theologico-Political Treatise' in *The Chief Works of Benedict de Spinoza*, VOL. 1 (New York: Dover, 1951), pp. 81–97.

these—a solely human power, a radical doubt about the constituted power, political atheism—not some of the characteristics that define the anti-state Action of the Multitude?

In general, the fact that Hobbes and Schmitt assign the Miracle to the sovereign does not in any way run counter to the connection between Action and Miracle, and rather somehow confirms it; for these authors, it is indeed *only* the sovereign who acts politically. The point is therefore not to deny the importance of the state of exception in the name of a critique of sovereignty, but to understand what form the state of exception can take once political Action is in the hands of the Many. Insurrections, desertions, invention of new democratic organizations, and application of the principle of the *tertium datur*: these are the Miracles of the Multitude, those who do not cease when the sovereign forbids them.

However, in opposition to Arendt, miraculous exception is not a rootless and completely imponderable event. Insofar as it is triggered within the magnetic field defined by the changing relations of Action with Labour and the Intellect, the Miracle is rather an *expected unforeseen*. As happens in every oxymoron, the two terms are in reciprocal tension yet indivisible. If only a redemptive unforeseen or a forward-looking expectation were in question, we would deal, respectively, with the most meaningless randomness or a banal calculation of the relationship between means and ends. Instead, this is an exception that surprises especially those who have been waiting for it: an anomaly that is sufficiently precious and powerful to get out of play the conceptual bearings that nonetheless signalled the place of its onset; a discrepancy between causes and effects of which we can always grasp the cause, without for this reason weakening its innovative effect.

Eventually, it is precisely the explicit reference to an *expected unforeseen*—the exhibition of a necessary incompleteness—that constitutes the badge of honour of every political theory that disdains the benevolence of the sovereign.

THE USE OF LIFE

To Valerij Pavlovič

1.

Touch

With respect to use, touch prevails to the detriment of sight (the *the-orein* or contemplative-theoretical gaze). The visual object faces us from a given distance—it is independent from the observer and liable to a disinterested recognition. Use never has to do with something that stands in front of us, and hence with an object in the strict sense, opposed to the I. Whether it is words, clothes, a period of time, or a theorem, what we use is adjacent, lateral, and capable of friction. The used thing retroacts on the living being that uses it, transforming its conduct. This same reflexivity characterizes tactile experience: when we touch a branch, we are in turn touched by the branch we are touching.

Neither use nor touch explain the typical properties of an entity, but grasp its *appropriateness* (or vice versa, refractoriness) to an ongoing activity. Use is thoroughly marked by *interest* in the most literal meaning of the term: *inter-esse*, being-between, that is, the incorporation into a relationship that impinges on the autonomy of the correlated poles. Taking interest in the tool he uses, the agent cannot be adequately defined without mentioning this tool, even though it does not add anything to his nature or essence.

2.

Prepositions

The linguistic equivalent of use is not to be found in the attribution of a predicate to a grammatical subject. Unsaid or distorted by names and verbs, tactile handling is instead expressed by prepositions. The latter link and sustain; they are the symbols of the *inter-esse*, and signal appropriateness and friction. Prepositions signify only the relationships that they themselves establish; they conform to a contingent situation, bringing to light what medieval grammarians called *circumstantiae rerum*; they document the way in which the words they precede are employed. Using something—for instance, a helicopter or an ironic statement—means using it *to* a certain end; *in* a specific context; *for* the purpose of exhibiting an ability or role; *with* the assistance of multiple gestures; *among* friends or strangers; *from* a certain place.

Speakers use names and verbs like any other tool. But prepositions account for use as such, which is moreover the kind of use that, according to Wittgenstein, determines the meaning of names and verbs. The thought of use is a *prepositional thought*.

Note

Assuming for a moment that use forges the meaning of every word, we still need to ask what the meaning of the word 'use' is. Should we answer that it also depends on the way in which we use this word, we would fall into a vicious circle or an infinite regression. What specifies in detail the meaning of 'use' is instead the functioning of those terms that—devoid of an autonomous semantic content—participate in forming and varying every kind of semantic content, namely, 'for', 'with', 'in', 'between', *'katà'*, *'durch'*, etc. Prepositions are the empirical reality and the polytheistic double of use; use is the idea, or common name, of prepositions.

3.
Wax Tablet

Use is the basic activity from which production (*poiesis*) and political action (*praxis*) originate. Since it is the source of both it cannot be equated with either of them. Its peculiar trait is the indistinction between *poiesis* and *praxis*, or also, which is the same, their inextricable blend. The use of a plot of land or of an information is 'political' to the precise extent to which it is also 'productive', and vice versa. According to Aristotle, *poiesis* relies on technique (*techne*), while *praxis* counts on wisdom (*phronesis*—a term that, benefiting from the title of a Spike Lee movie, could better be rendered as 'the ability to do the right thing'). Now, in the use of a plot of land or of an information, *techne* is always imbued with wisdom just as *phronesis* is imbued with technique. It would be terribly wrong to criticize production and politics in the name of use. Use does indeed differ from production and politics, but only because it is their common premise. We need to be incredibly naïve to believe that A, the background and condition of possibility for B and C, is a kind of Chronos devoted to destroying his sons, that is, discrediting and eradicating B and C. We thus carelessly confuse the as yet unspecified matrix of every operation with the emblem of an inoperative existence. Rest assured that rentiers and mediocre intellectuals who boast about their non-involvement with political conflicts will be clapping.

Let us now shift our attention from use as an activity to the enti-
ties to which it applies. Another distinction dear to the philosophical
tradition withers away in the way of being of usable things, namely,
that between potency and act. The kitchen, computer, or dictionary
we use again and again are undoubtedly actualized realities, endowed
with an unmistakable form, and far from latent. But their actuality,
or presence, has a lot in common with the actuality, or presence, of
a wax tablet on which we can write any text. Usable things are acts
in which an as yet unaccomplished potency is embodied, one that is
never fully exhausted by the collection of its prospective accomplish-
ments. Usable things *reify* this potency, exhibiting its incompleteness
in their concrete spatiotemporal existence. However, they reify it
without actualizing it. I would argue that usable things are the *reality
of the possible*; but it is also necessary to add that this possible stub-
bornly remains such. It is well known that the statement on which
the paradox of the liar is based ('I lie') is false if it is true and true if
it is false. Similarly, if the kitchen, computer, and dictionary—as
closely related to the wax tablet—are considered as acts they soon
appear as potencies; but if they are understood as potencies they soon
prove their nature of acts. Instead of alternating in time, the two
canonical notions of *dynamis* and *energeia* converge and overlap. We
should here think of the ambivalent figures studied by Gestalt psychology; in one and the same tangle of lines, we can discern both
the image of a rabbit and that of a duck. Every entity subjected to
use is at the same time duck and rabbit.

Note

Over the last decades the process of capitalist accumulation increasingly—
and at times preponderantly—relies on resources that can be used repeatedly by many subjects without losing any of their initial consistency—such
as knowledge, inventions, communication technologies, etc. This explains
why the current production of commodities often displays the combination
of *poiesis* and *praxis*—job performance and political action—that is the

distinguishing mark of the activity of use. It explains why the tasks one is allocated in a factory or office require as much *phronesis* as *techne*. It also explains why the raw material on which we intervene is a reified potency, the reality of the possible, or a wax tablet. Geared towards a repeated and plural use, epistemic and linguistic resources are however captured, computed, and exchanged as if they were goods that are consumable only once and by an individual subject. Just to be clear: biological knowledge is treated like a cubic metre of gas, of which nothing remains after it is burnt. In this way political economy—which is a science of scarcity—governs phenomena that most contradict it and even turns them into its genuine cornerstone. This systematic equivocation, thanks to which use is transfigured into consumption, is the focal point of contemporary capitalism, but also a hotbed for its permanent crisis.

4.

What the Human Being Can Do of Himself

We use cars, shoes, and maps with a view to our life, its preservation, and strengthening. But what is first of all usable is the very life with a view to which we use cars, shoes and maps. The presupposition and foundation of every use is the *use of the self*, of our existence.

The relation we entertain with our life is always tactile and not at all visual. It is never the case that life stands out as an object that faces us, which we could investigate and represent. As not an end in itself and open to dissimilar usages [*utilizzazioni*], the human animal perceives life as something within reach, that looms over and drives us, and by which we are touched at the precise moment when we touch it.

Foucault's great merit is to have shown that in the classical world the all too celebrated precept *gnothi seauton*—'know thyself'—was only a late corollary, and even a distortion, of the far more fundamental *epimeleia heautou*—the use and care of the self. While the *gnothi* implies a pre-eminence of vision—the *theorein* with which an imperturbable subject scrutinizes an object that stands in front of him—the *epimeleia* is entirely contained within a manual probing. It is not so much a matter of studying one's faculties (perception, memory, imagination, etc.) as of perfecting the way we use them. Instead of describing what the human being is, it is necessary to advance what he can do with himself thanks to a daily exercise whose least defective name is perhaps *spiel* or *play*—game and performance at the same time.

Note

The use of life is closely linked to the use of language. The *epimeleia heautou*, the care of the self, is unconceivable without the *epimeleia logou*, the care of one's discourses—and, of course, vice versa. A remark made by Wittgenstein helps us to clarify this matter:

> 'It is always for living beings that signs exist, so that must be something essential to a sign.' Yes, but how is a living being defined? It appears that here I am prepared to use its capacity to use a sign-language as a defining mark of a living being. And the concept of a living being really has an indeterminacy very similar to that of the concept of 'language'.[1]

In order to explain what a linguistic sign is I need to dwell on the way in which a living being employs it; in order to explain what a living being is I need to mention its inclination to use linguistic signs. Referring to and mutually sustaining one another, the two terms—life and logos—reveal their common *indeterminacy*. Now, it is precisely indeterminacy that makes use possible, and even inevitable. Both life and language are indeed usable because they are undetermined; both require an uninterrupted modulation in order to be detailed in well-articulated scores and scripts (habits, roles, jargons, rhetorical tropes). Prepositions as the most undetermined component of language provide for expressing this double usability.

Following Wittgenstein's refrain, use establishes and subsequently modifies verbal meanings, but we should bear in mind that this is the speakers' *use of life*. The latter is realized also in discourses, but can certainly not be limited to them. The semantic content of 'painting', 'love', 'sanctity',

---

1 Ludwig Wittgenstein, *Philosophical Grammar* (Berkeley and Los Angeles: University of California Press, 1974), p. 192.

'money', 'addition', etc., does not depend so much on the way in which we use these terms as on the interweaving of linguistic and non-linguistic activities in which the usage of our existence is unfolded. Stanley Cavell wrote that 'you cannot use words to do what we do with them until you are initiate of the forms of life which give those words the point and shape they have in our lives.'[2] This is correct provided that we understand 'forms of life' as nothing more and nothing less than the different uses life is subject to.

---

2 Stanley Cavell, *The Claim of Reason: Wittgenstein, Skepticism, Morality, and Tragedy* (Oxford: Oxford University Press, 1999), p. 184.

5.
The Clumsy Animal

The use of the self is founded on the detachment from the self. It is embedded in the failed inherence to the environment in which we are nonetheless situated and to the psychic drives that master us at each turn. What is used is an existence with which we do not always identify ourselves, which we do not fully own, and which is not fully familiar—although it is certainly not alien. The use of life appears where life is presented as a task and, at the same time, as the tool that enables us to fulfil this task. In other words, the use of life belongs to the species that, in addition to living, should make its life possible.

In deploying its own body, the human animal is *clumsy*, exposed to error and misfires. In a recent debate, an influential philosopher claimed that this defective character, which is absent in other animals, does not prevent us to extend the use of the self to the case of man. I disagree. I think that we can speak with good reason of the use of the self *only* (and hence not 'also' or 'even') with regard to a clumsy being, marked by a partial ineptitude, and doomed to uncertainty. The living being detached from itself, who never fully coincides with its works and days, is clumsy and neotenic (that is, chronically immature). But, as I just said, it is actually this detachment and this non-coincidence that enable the use of life.

6.

Having

Stating that the human animal retains a detachment from its own life, the drives that animate it, and the language in which it dwells, is the same as stating that the human animal *is* not this life, these drives, and this language, but *has* them. Unlike the verb 'to be', 'to have' expresses a relation of belonging that, however, resolutely rules out the identity between the terms involved in it. It is precisely the deficiency of identification with the talents we have at our disposal that opens up the possibility of using them irreverently. We use only what we have, and never what is consubstantial with us to the point that we cannot distinguish ourselves from it.

In his essay 'The Linguistic Functions of "to be" and "to have"', Émile Benveniste observes that the verb 'to have', which many languages lack, originates from the previous and much more widespread construction 'y is to x'—for instance, 'the coat is to Giovanni'. The standard *habeo aliquid*, 'I have something,' is nothing other than 'a secondary and derivative variant' of *mihi est aliquid*, 'something is to me.'[1] The philosophical importance of 'to have' is fully brought to

---

1 Émile Benveniste, 'The Linguistic Functions of "to be" and "to have" ' in *Problems in General Linguistics* (Miami: Miami University Press, 1971), p. 172.

light as soon as we refer it back to the 'being-to' from which it derives. The logical subject—the one who has—loses his prominent position, sanctioned by the nominative case, and adapts to the role of comple-ment in the dative case; he does not sustain or introduce anything but is instead sustained and introduced by the preposition 'to'—or also the preposition 'at' (in Russian, 'I have the book' becomes *u menja est' kniga*, 'the book is at me').

The cases in which the construction 'y is to x' highlights a requirement that contributes to defining the nature of x are of great interest—that is to say, one of those requirements in the absence of which x would instantly disappear. Let us consider the phrase Aristotle coined to designate our species:[2] *zoon logon echon*, the animal that *has* language, that is, the animal *to* which (or *at* which) language is. Let us also consider the hypothesis that works as the North Star of Helmuth Plessner's philosophical anthropology;[3] the human being *has* a body instead of being limited to existing as a body; it *has* it because it can treat it as a tool, act with and on it, and use it for the most different purposes. One of Osip Mandelstam's early poems opens with a similar observation full of wonder: 'I was given a body [*Dano mne telo*]—What shall I do with this gift, so much my own and unique?'[4] What is at stake in Aristotle's phrase and Plessner's hypoth-esis is not a having that is added to the essence of the *Homo sapiens* primate (as instead happens with the statements 'the cold was to the mountaineer' and 'fear was at the soldier'), but a having that consti-tutes the kernel of such an essence. Far from being idiosyncratic, the reference to the verb 'to have' indicates with precision the relation-ship the human animal establishes with its distinctive dispositions. Insofar as they are *to* it, language, the body, emotions, imagination,

---

2 Aristotle, *Politics* 1253a9–10.

3 Helmuth Plessner, *Laughing and Crying. A Study of the Limits of Human Behavior* (Evanston, IL: Northwestern University Press, 1970).

4 Osip Mandelstam, *Kamen* (Peterburg: Akme, 1913).

and even life are presented as something unavoidable, certain, but also *extrinsic*. The 'being-to' corrodes the hegemony of the copula 'is'. While 'x is y' (for instance, 'man is language') proclaims the symbiotic unity of subject and predicate, 'y is to x' ('language is to man') uncovers a gap, or at least an imperfect fusion, between the attribute and the entity to which it applies. Obviously, the gap in question does not entail that the *Homo sapiens* primate is able to separate itself from its nature or remould it at will, but that this nature—which is neither ephemeral nor variable—is prearranged from the outset for dissimilar uses [*utilizzazioni*].

We use what we have. The human animal, *at* which life and language are, never stops using them. It *has*, and therefore uses, its essence. But using one's essence (*ousia* or *quid est* in classical philosophy) is not different from using oneself. In 'y is *to* (or *at*) x', both y and x refer to one and the same subject, for instance, a woman named Raissa. What varies is only the aspect to which the reference is addressed; while y denotes Raissa as a set of *usable* inclinations and qualities, x signals instead, in Raissa, the *capacity to use* the inclinations and qualities that are *to* her. Here the two specular meanings of the Latin adjective *habilis* (which not without reason directly derives from *habere*, 'to have') coexist and interact—'lending oneself to be used' and, on the contrary, 'being able to use'. This adjective suits both a comfortable and bold skirt and the one who knows how to wear it with calculated nonchalance. The use of the self is reserved to the living being that, *having* its essence, is *habilis* in both senses of the term.

7.
Institutional Phenomena

The use [*utilizzazione*] of one's existence, which is a prerogative and duty of the clumsy animal, requires training, protracted exercise, experimental procedures, technical acquisitions, and the observance of rules. The uses of the self are not instinctive, natural or spontaneous. At most, they *become* such: their easiness is nothing other than a difficulty that was overcome; the grace that at times characterizes them lets us obliquely glimpse the original awkwardness.

The training, techniques, and rules that nourish the inclination to use one's life constitute the anthropological (that is, meta-historical) foundation of institutions. Better said, they are the pervasive and manifold *institutional phenomena* that are organized as actual institutions only under certain conditions and never fully. It goes without saying that institutional phenomena—the 'technologies of the self' investigated by Foucault[1]—are a battlefield and not a liberated territory. This field remains almost unaltered, like our upright position and faculty of language, but the outcomes of the battle are variable and surprising. The stakes of class struggles are the way in which we use life. They do not fail to invent unprecedented habits [*usanze*],

---

1 Michel Foucault, *Technologies of the Self: A Seminar with Michel Foucault* (Amherst, MA: The University of Massachusetts Press, 1988).

capable of confining those that had prevailed to the museum of horrors. Modifying the traditional forms of the *epimeleia heautou*, they can generate institutions on a collision course with state sovereignty and the buying and selling of labour power, with the Ministry of the Interior and the International Monetary Fund.

The use of life avails itself of techniques and always has an institutional aspect. It is even legitimate to suppose that it lies at the origin of the notions of 'technique' and 'institution'. Consequently, the use of the self and of surrounding things is never exempt from rules. Adopting Wittgenstein's jargon, it is never devoid of a grammar. In order to avoid misunderstandings, it is here necessary to introduce a conceptual distinction. The *rules* are not juridical *norms*. Between the two there is not only a logical unevenness but also an irreducible contrast. The rule is one with use; it animates it and is animated by it; it does not subsist outside of it. We could say that the use [*utilizzazione*] of life is, at the same time, an activity requiring a measurement and a unit of measurement, a conduct to be controlled and an instrument of control. On the contrary, the juridical norm is separated from use, postulates its (real or hypothetical) suspension, transcends it, surreptitiously applies to it criteria derived from the exchange of commodities (such as the equivalence of the exchanged products, the punishment of the debtor, the compensation of the creditor, etc.).

Those who equate rules [*regole*] with norms, ignoring their belligerent heterogeneity, believe that use could elude and dismiss the sphere of right in virtue of its *unruliness* [*sregolatezza*], that is, insofar as it would remain immune to every kind of bonding grammar. This is a pernicious illusion. The varied deployment of our existence is alien to juridical norms, and at times even manages to undermine them, only because it benefits from rules at every step. The imperatives of the law struggle to tighten their grip on collective behaviours where the provisions and unity of measurement of a grammar apply. If we underestimate the centrality of rules in the use of the self, we—knowingly or unknowingly—helplessly yield to the domination of norms.

8.

The Pronoun 'We'

Far from privileging solitude, the use of the self is inscribed from the outset in the public sphere, bringing together the individual living being with a more or less extensive multitude of peers. It is an *institutional phenomenon* (a permanent building block of institutions in the strict sense of the term, which are as such inclined to every kind of metamorphosis) also and especially for this reason. Neither anonymous nor internal, the use of the self gives rise to the pronoun 'we'.

Unpopular with sophisticated philosophers since it symbolizes unbridled working class insurrections and speaks for the sordid complicity among the oppressed, this pronoun is located half-way between the first grammatical person—the 'I' that takes the floor— and the other two persons—the 'you' to whom speech is addressed and the 'he' that remains alien to the enunciation underway. Émile Benveniste observes that 'we' 'is not a multiplication of identical objects, but a junction between "I" and "non-I"'.[1] The 'non-I' implicit in the 'we' can assume two different aspects: 'me + you (plural)' or 'me + them'. In the first case, the 'we' attests to the unity of the 'I'

---

1 Benveniste, 'Relationships of Persons in the Verb' in *Problems in General Linguistics*, p. 202.

with a plurality of 'you' present at the same time ('you' plural); in the second case, the 'we' indicates instead the increasing convergence between the 'I' and a set of 'he' that are for the moment absent ('they').

What prevails in the use [*utilizzazione*] of life, which always hinges on the 'we', is at times the familiar proximity of the 'me + you (plural)' and at others the distance not devoid of unknowns (and risks) of the 'me + them'. However, in both instances 'this "we" is something other than a junction of definable elements [. . .] The reason for this is that "we" is not a quantified or multiplied "I"; it is *an "I" expanded beyond the strict limits of the person*, enlarged and at the same time amorphous.'[2] What each of us does with his own body is certainly to be attributed to an 'I', but this is an 'I' that, giving free rein to the drives and the pre-individual faculties that are in it, is about to give up the metaphysical and juridical role of the person. The 'we' indicates the passage from the singular to the common, as well as from the common to the singular. It is a dynamic sign, a commutator, and a threshold. It delineates a no-man's-land in which neither the vain 'I' nor the irresponsible 'one' can lay claim to property rights. It is precisely in this no-man's-land that the *epimeleia heautou* dwells.

Being singular and common at the same time, the use of the self is conveyed in the best possible way by two phrases of the French vernacular. In Northern France we find a paradoxical, yet enlightening, *je sommes*, 'I are'. In Franco-Provençal, we encounter its specular equivalent, *nous suis*, 'we am'.[3] The deployment of one's existence, interwoven with techniques and rules, is an institutional phenomenon whose motto goes more or less like this: *I who use, we who uses* [*io usiamo, noi uso*].

---

2 Benveniste, 'Relationships of Persons in the Verb', p. 203 (emphasis added).
3 Benveniste, 'Relationships of Persons in the Verb', p. 203.

9.
Limits and Crisis of Use

We do not understand anything of the clumsy animal's use of life if we overlook the burden of the *disused*, the disconcerting contact with the *unusual*, and the ever-looming possibility of the *abuse*. These three negative notions, which change historically with regard to their content, are nonetheless always present in the *epimeleia heautou*. They follow like a shadow successful (that is, obvious and automatic) use, confer on it an unmistakable physiognomy, and, all in all, contribute to its definition.

Life is at the same time *activity of use* (to which the indistinction between production and political action applies) and *usable thing* (qualified by the juxtaposition of act and potency). Both a particular aspect of the usable thing that life is and one of the ways in which life manifests itself as an activity of use deserve to be labelled 'disused' and 'unusual'. However, here I will leave aside the difference between these two possibilities and limit myself to some general considerations.

'Disused' refers to an obsolete employment of our energies and talents, which is no longer practiced, and has even become bizarre. Only its techniques and rule—its grammar—remain. But insofar as it is separated from real use, this grammar is reduced to a psychological relic. The form of life that suffers from being disused is similar to a wax tablet entirely covered by a dense web of words; it is an act but no longer a potency.

'Unusual' refers to our as yet sporadic and undecided self-employment [*impiego di noi stessi*]. There is already a premonition of use, but only a premonition, since the techniques and rules that are an indispensable component of real use are still missing. In the light of unusualness, life stands out as a host of fluctuating possibilities, or, if you prefer, of hypothetical and shattered sentences for the writing of which we seem not to have a wax tablet.

The disused and the unusual constitute the *limits* of use. These are temporal limits, given that the former embodies its past and the latter adumbrates its future. It is the present use of life that shapes the field of the disused and the unusual, thus establishing its own past and future. Hence these are *internal* limits, drawn only by what is being delimited. However, the disused and the unusual in turn determine a description of the process they circumscribe, that is, arrange the salient characteristics of the present use of life. In its daily manifestations, the use [*utilizzazione*] of our existence oscillates between two antipodes, and preserves conspicuous traces of both. At times, we happen to glimpse the appearance of the unusual in the disused, but also, the other way round, to recognize in what we are not yet able to handle the doppelganger, or at least the echo, of what we are no longer familiar with. In this way, we only exacerbate the oscillating movement that characterizes every aspect of the current employment of our life.

While, on the one hand, the disused and the unusual are the (temporal) limits within which the use of the self takes place, on the other, abuse dictates its *crisis*. Let us be clear; a gesture or sentence is not abusive on the basis of a juridical norm. What is rather at stake is the contrast between two sides of use itself that are never separable, namely, its being at the same time a unit of measurement and a measured reality; a yardstick and a body endowed with an empirical length; a complex of rules and a contingent behaviour to which rules are applied. The inseparability of the two sides does not at all entail their harmony. Abuse is a move in the use of life that contradicts, or oversteps, those rules without which it would not be . . . a move in the use of life. The abusive move can be inhibited in the name of the rules it embodies, but can also contribute to modifying these rules. In both cases, we are dealing with the crisis of ordinary use—a crisis whose possibility accompanies the *epimeleia heautou* like a basso continuo. The use of life is nothing other than a curbed abuse or, alternatively, an abuse that is promoted in order to form a new grammar.

Finally, we should here hint at radical abuse. It amounts to suspending, or even abrogating, use as such, transforming it into something different; for instance, a purely productive conduct (pure *poiesis*), or a purely political conduct (a non-hybridized *praxis*). A *techne* without *phronesis* and a *phronesis* without *techne* are abusive. The passage from the use of life to its voracious or indolent consumption is itself utterly abusive. Consumed life resembles a barrel of oil or food, that is, goods that are annihilated at the very moment when they are enjoyed; used life has instead much in common with a language and a writing desk as things that preserve their potency long after we use them.

10.

The Care of the Self

According to Foucault, the use of life requires a continuous care of
the self. The reason for this is easy to grasp: we could not effectively
avail ourselves of our existence, if we did not adopt, day after day,
the necessary measures to turn it into a well-tempered, ductile, and
polyvalent instrument. Those who arrange their psychophysical
organism for the most various employments, taking care of guaranteeing its constant handiness, can be said to be accurate.

In the lessons published under the title of *The Hermeneutics of the
Subject*,[1] Foucault analyses the forms taken by the care of the self in
Hellenistic society and in early Christianity. Well-known examples
include soul-searching; the epistolary account made to a friend of
the excesses and shortcomings that permeated the afternoon one has
just spent; the mental experiments on the different ways to react to
an unexpected event; ascetic precepts; confession; the careful administration of a vocation or skill; counterfactual reasoning ('if I were
not the musician or courtesan I actually am, then I would act in such
and such a way'); the training in performing the role of different characters in human comedy; the conjectural evocation of emotions one

---

1 Michel Foucault, *The Hermeneutics of the Subject: Lectures at the Collège de
France 1981–1982* (London: Palgrave Macmillan, 2005).

currently does not share; the readiness to move between thoroughly heterogeneous kinds of discourse. What do we obtain from this list (and its virtual continuation)? What is, after all, the kernel of the concept of care?

It is striking that the practices into which flow the preoccupation about one's usability in turn amount to a peculiar use [*utilizzazione*] of the self. The care, which prepares us for every sort of tactile handling of life, is *already* as such a way in which the living being touches and handles oneself. Rather than a preamble to use, the care is its reflexive redoubling. Testing our psychophysical organism through simulations and experiments, *we use this organism in order to make it always more usable*. In short, the care is a use to the power of two. Soul-searching, asceticism, counterfactual reasoning, etc., are packed with techniques and rules whose eminent function is to facilitate the acquisition of techniques and rules on which the manifold particular uses of our existence depend.

The care of the self is the most primordial way of using life. And yet, in the care, life as a *usable thing* fully coincides with life as a *capacity to use*; reciprocally, the capacity to use is presented from the outset in the guise of a usable thing. What we aim at handling by means of spiritual exercises, or the effort to identify ourselves with imaginary situations, is nothing other than our very tendency to handle: 'The care of the self is the care of the soul as an activity principle and not as a substance.'[2] When it is itself treated as a usable thing, the capacity to use (as synonymous with the 'activity principle' of which Foucault speaks) is condensed into customs [*usanze*], that is, a complex of habits, dispositions and postures.

The customs generated by the care—by that use of existence that aims at enhancing the faculty of making use of existence—are the field in which we *enjoy* ourselves (the 'we' that refers to both 'me + you (plural)' and 'me + them'). In *On Christian Doctrine*, Augustine of Hippo opposes the *uti*—the use of something with a view to

---

2 Foucault, *Technologies of the Self*, p. 25.

something else—to the *frui*—the enjoyment of an object for what it is, without any extrinsic finality. He wonders 'whether men should enjoy themselves, use, or do both'.[3] In customs, the *uti* and the *frui* neither destroy each other nor blend. In spite of their discrepancy, using and enjoying intersect like two perpendicular lines. When it is consolidated into habits and dispositions, the care of the self includes both the *enjoyment of use* (or better, of the capacity to use) and the *use of enjoyment*. The lasting difference between *uti* and *frui* does not rule out—and even allows for and supports—the application of the *uti* to the *frui* and of the *frui* to the *uti*—a chiasmic relation.

Note

In the age of capitalism, the life to be used is presented as labour-power. This term designates the power to produce. Or better, it designates all the physical and mental powers inherent in the human body (the faculty of language, motor skills, memory, inclination to learn, etc.), provided that they are addressed to production. Bought and sold even before it is actualized in specific work operations, the *dynamis* that bears the name 'labour-power' is the point to which the modern care of the self is applied. We need to safeguard, qualify, and enhance our power to produce, that is, our usability within capitalist enterprise. The care of the self that prepares the use of the self by others is incessant and even frenetic.

The 'hermeneutics of the subject', punctuated by spiritual exercises and role games, is by now an integral part of the concept of labour-power. And it greatly contributes to determining the exchange value of the latter. Soul-searching, the study of the ways in which one has to react to an unexpected event, training to perform different scripts, and even confession, resurface in internships and refresher courses, that is, in the 'lifelong learning' that is imposed on waged workers. The care of the soul practiced by the Stoics and early Christian communities finds a grotesque—yet not unfaithful—equivalent in the cautious and circumspect behaviour of the tramps of the earth who indulge in the infamous mythology according to which each of them would be a 'self-entrepreneur'.

---

3 Augustine of Hippo, *On Christian Doctrine*, 1.20.

11.

On Stage

Acting recapitulates and amplifies the procedures through which the clumsy animal—the animal that never fully identifies with the actions and passions it experiences—avails itself of its existence. The activity of the actor is an unmatched model for the use of life and the care of the self. The philosophical reflection on the *epimeleia heautou* culminates in the theories (which are actually very distant from philosophical torments and idiosyncrasies) that have dissected this activity, examining each of its articulations. The writings of Stanislavsky, Meyerhold, Brecht and Grotowski are more instructive than the works of Marcus Aurelius and Tertullian. In order to precisely reconstruct the 'technologies of the self', we need to examine the techniques ham actors and star performers resort to when they stage and play a tragedy or a comedy.

The care of the self, aimed at guaranteeing and perfecting the usability of our psychophysical organism, is unfolded in an exceptionally clear way in the period of time during which the actor becomes familiar with the character he is about to interpret. In view of a future performance on stage, he works assiduously on himself, and challenges himself with improvisations, introspective scrutiny, tests devised by the imagination, variations of gestures and diction.

According to Stanislavsky,[1] for those who are preparing to use themselves in front of an audience nothing is more important than 'living through' (*perezhivanie*), that is, retrieving in one's own biographical experience events and states of mind analogous to those that mark the character's fate. In order to unfold the game of analogies, it is necessary that the actor study, travel, attend art exhibitions and cheap bars, and collect the most different ways of living and speaking with the meticulousness of a botanist. Furthermore, Stanislavsky believes that the performer preliminarily needs to divide the role he was assigned—the way in which he will use his body on stage—into a series of particular 'tasks' (*zadachi*); stroking a childish toy during a nostalgic monologue; insinuating with a grimace that one should not trust that courteous man; staring at the sky as if one were waiting for an impossible revelation. It goes without saying that 'living through' and the individuation of tasks that are appropriate to the circumstances are only examples—chosen almost randomly—of the 'technologies of the self' exhibited by acting.

Considered as a whole, the training undergone by the actor in the phase that precedes the staging of a play only prolongs and intensifies the *meditatio* of the Stoics. As a pivotal point of the care of the self, the *meditatio* amounts to imagining oneself in a fictitious situation one has to learn how to cope with; all in all, it is a matter of becoming the one who dies, enjoys, fights on the barricades, or sinks into despair. Thanks to this mental projection, we become familiar with the roles that sooner or later we will have to perform, elaborating in advance the appropriate gestures and lines. The *meditatio* is an acting exercise without witnesses; acting exercises are a public *meditatio*, which presupposes from the outset the involvement of the spectators. The inoperative actor embodies a generic capacity to use himself; if you wish, he is a 'for', 'with', 'between', and 'in' not as yet inserted in a

---

1 Konstantin Stanislavsky, *An Actor's Work on a Role* (London: Routledge, 2010).

meaningful sentence. Instead, the actor undergoing training—not unlike the Stoic devoted to the *meditatio*—starts to apply the free-value prepositions of which he is a bearer to determined phrases ('the escape of King Lear'; 'the excoriating disappointment that is awaiting me').

Note

In contemporary theatre, training—the care of the self—often amounts to the ultimate goal of the actor's activity. He prepares for a staging that is always postponed, only hypothetical, and in any case inessential. Grotowski's school has exacerbated this propensity to separate the endless enhancement of one's usability from every actual use [*utilizzazione*]. Like a ballet dancer content with his daily barre work, or a singer longing only to continue his propaedeutic vocalizing, the actor harbours a profound disgust for passing from rehearsals to the performance. The gap between training and contingent implementation, care and use of the self, is a distinctive trait of current forms of life. The figure of the actor interested exclusively in training mirrors the inhabitant of a big city who, wishing to remain always available to every possible role (that of the bohemian as well as that of the successful computer scientist or—why not?—the intransigent revolutionary), steers clear of any univocal interpretation. But this analogy is too vague. I will propose another—more circumscribed—one, and I would not know whether it is alternative or complementary to the former. The actor's predilection for a training process independent from staging a play is shared, on a larger scale, by precarious intellectual labour; it is in fact well known that the relative autonomy the intellectual worker enjoys in the acquisition and enrichment of his linguistic-cognitive skills is doomed to turn into absolute subordination as soon as capitalist enterprise really uses them. The contrast between training and performance is perhaps the seismograph of forthcoming future conflicts. The demand to experience a different use of life—that is, innovative ways to be on stage—surfaces in the unprecedented inflation of the care of the self.

12.

Estrangement Effect

The source of every use of the self—above all, the use of the self that takes place in acting—is a persistent detachment from the self. Only the living being that struggles to identify with the actions it carries out and the words it utters is able to use its life as a tool; it alone has the faculty of interpreting one or the other character in front of an audience. Showing considerable philosophical acumen, Bertolt Brecht intended to stage the condition that makes possible every staging (as well as, in general, every use of life), namely, the detachment from the self. Instead of remaining the concealed foundation of his professional performance, the non-identification with what he does and says must be exhibited by the actor without reservations. Distancing oneself from a role is an unavoidable component of playing it. Brecht called this distancing *Verfremdungseffekt*, that is, 'estrangement effect'. The *Verfremdungseffekt*—which refined philosophers ridicule as an old and tasteless piece of junk—brings out the obscure source of the use of the self, or, more emphatically, gives empirical appearance to the transcendental presupposition of such a use. This is quite something.

The ability of the Brechtian actor rests with conferring an unnatural, and even unsettling, aspect upon events, behaviours, and ways of thinking with which the spectators are absolutely familiar.

The transformation of what is habitual-reassuring into a set of surprising-threatening phenomena resembles to some extent to the metamorphosis from which, according to Freud, the feeling of the uncanny originates. However, there is a difference; in Brecht's theatre, what becomes alien and frightening is the *current* social and political reality, and not a *remote* protection which we enjoyed in our infancy. While the uncanny investigated by Freud has a diachronic structure (what used to be habitual now returns with a threatening aspect), the uncanny Brecht intends to produce anew, thanks to the *Verfremdungseffekt*, is rigorously synchronic (what turns out to be threatening is precisely what now stands as habitual).

In order to obtain the estrangement effect, the actor utters his lines as if they were citations in inverted commas, without any kind of identification, and even adopting the 'attitude of a person who is astounded and contradicts himself'.[1] He also suggests in all possible ways that the decisions taken by the character are not the only conceivable ones: '[He] will act in such a way that the alternative emerges as clearly as possible; that [his] acting allows the other possibilities to be inferred and only represents one out of the possible variants. [. . .] Whatever he does *not* do must be contained and preserved in what he does.'[2] In order to highlight the historical content of the narrated facts—their transience—the actor pretends to be looking at them retrospectively, showing he knows what happened next.[3] Brecht writes that 'it is up to the actors to treat present-day events and modes of behaviour with the same detachment as historians adopt with regard to those of the past.'[4] In *Theses on the Philosophy of History*, when he enjoins the materialist historian not to identify with the age

---

1 Bertolt Brecht, 'Short Description of a New Technique of Acting that Produces a *Verfremdung* Effect' in *Brecht on Theatre* (London: Bloomsbury, 2015), p. 185.

2 Brecht, 'Short Description', p. 185.

3 See Bertolt Brecht, 'Short Organon for the Theatre' in *Brecht on Theatre*, Sections 50–51.

4 Brecht, 'Short Description', p. 188.

he studies, to point out the unrealized possibilities it was fraught with, and to take into account the developments that have taken place after its decline, Walter Benjamin is not parroting some insipid Messianic thought of Scholem, but fully drawing on Brecht's theses on acting.

What model of the use of the self can be deduced from the performance of an actor capable of giving rise to the estrangement effect? How does distancing oneself from the role one is interpreting affect the *epimeleia heautou*? What does it mean to use one's life by continuously exhibiting, by means of appropriate techniques, the condition that makes possible every use of life, that is, non-identification with what one does and says? It seems to me that the *Verfremdungseffekt* locates the use of the self near its *limits*, namely, the disused and the unusual. And that it also renders palpable the *crisis*, or abuse, use is always exposed to. When he adopts the 'attitude of a person who is astounded' by the lines he is reciting, or alludes to the alternative behaviours his character could have displayed, the Brechtian actor treats the lines he declaims and the actual conduct of the character as something that is no longer or not yet used, or as something that violates the rules on which use depends. However, estrangement does not entail that the actor refrains from representing well-defined events or human types, being satisfied with formulating some wise comments. Even though (and, for Brecht, precisely because) he does not identify with their vicissitudes, he will be a touching Uncle Vanya and a memorable Macbeth. Likewise, a use of life that takes distance from itself, revealing its disused, unusual, or abusive physiognomy, does not at all cease to be a determined and contingent use of life. Far from weakening determinateness and contingency, the distancing disproportionally emphasizes them. The non-identification with what one does and says at each turn becomes a constitutive element of *this* doing and *this* saying. Being neither Hellenistic nor Proto-Christian, the training to make use of even the limits and crisis of use rather characterizes the *epimeleia heautou* of the contemporary materialist. The estrangement effect is his spiritual exercise.

13.
Wittgenstein's Director's Notes

The use of the self consists of an interweaving of linguistic and non-linguistic activities, discourses and tacit gestures, questions and physical scuffles, prayers and kneeling. In this respect too, acting is a formidable handbook of the ways in which the clumsy animal uses its own existence. In fact, the centre of gravity of the actor's performance lies in the—always problematic—correlation between the lines in his script and the movements or physiognomic expressions of the one who utters them. The fragility of affects that seemed eternal can be evoked on stage only if the words 'it's all going to be alright' are accompanied by a plain spreading out of the arms. Obviously, the same applies to the representation of surprise and boredom, or the announcement that dinner is ready.

There is more to it. Putting on a play is the laboratory in which the interweaving of discourses and gestures characterizing the use of life is *broken down*. Preparing to interpret his part, the actor emulates the chemist; he artificially separates what is presented in nature as always combined, and even symbiotic. There is an initial phase in which he walks around, throws a punch, smiles, and runs away without saying anything; words are an obstacle for action, ruining its effectiveness and fluidity. According to Stanislavsky, during the first rehearsals [*prove*] the actor should refrain from uttering the lines of the text, and replace them with meaningless sounds, whistles, and monotonous 'ta-ta-ti'. Later on, the situation is reversed. Goethe's maxim 'in the beginning was action' gives way to St John's 'in the beginning was the word'. Now the word reigns over the entire scene; the movements and mimetic attitudes that were previously developed now seem to disturb the intensity of the dialogues. Sentences are exchanged in a state on inertia, without doing anything. It goes without saying that the actor-chemist eventually needs to reunify what he has thus far kept separate; at this point the lines become an aspect of gestures, and gestures an ingredient of the lines.

Suspending and then restoring the cooperation between linguistic and non-linguistic activities, the performer of the play brings to light the outline of the human form of life (or, which is the same, the outline of the use of life by the human animals). It also provides us with precious suggestions about a crucial passage of anthropogenesis. There are statements that struggle to be inserted into the sequence of gestures and movements, and non-verbal initiatives that find it difficult to be integrated within what is being said; everything points to the fact that this twofold difficulty for long marked the formation process of our species. The actor who sees in speech a hurdle for action, and in action a weakening of speech, reproduces on a small scale the evolutionary training of the speaking animal.

In the last twenty years of his life, Ludwig Wittgenstein never lost sight of the indissoluble link between speaking and acting, semantics and bodily motion. His field of research coincides to a large extent with the problems that torment the actors and directors during the preparation of a performance. Like theatre people, Wittgenstein himself analytically reconstructs the bond between statements and gestures by means of a host of experiments, or better, *tests* [*prove*]. For instance, he asks how we should picture the—only apparently simple—scene of a builder who orders his assistant to pass him the building-stones;[1] or what the verbal *and* physiognomic manifestations of doubt, waiting, and pain are. Wittgenstein calls these experimental tests *Sprachspiele*. The German term is rendered into English as 'language-games'. I would like to propose a different translation, namely, *linguistic performances*. This is a reasonable variant since the verb *spielen* means both 'to play' and 'to perform'. But this alternative translation presents also some benefits from an openly theoretical standpoint. In line of principle, a game can be exclusively verbal, a performance never. A game played with words is limited to presupposing certain non-linguistic practices; instead, a performance explicitly focuses on the intersection between these practices and discourses, witnessing to their inseparability. A game (for instance, listing the colours we know) stands out against the background of a form of life (that of the painter or the florist); a performance includes the alleged background, makes it visible, and highlights its figure (we list the colours *while* we put the last brush strokes to the painting or tie a bouquet).

Both Wittgenstein's linguistic performances and theatrical plays do not concede anything to the invisible. Psychological depth has no function in them. What happens on stage—that is, the reciprocal reference of discourses and actions—is more than enough to account for feelings, thoughts, intentions, desires, hypocrisies, sorrows and reluctances. The spectator does not need to suppose the influence of obscure mental states in order to understand Hamlet's conduct or that of Goldoni's Mistress of the Inn. Wittgenstein proves to have a genuine theatrical vocation when he writes that 'we *see* emotion.'[2] When we immediately grasp the happiness or anger of a person, we certainly do not move from a smiling or threatening face to an

---

1 Ludwig Wittgenstein, *Philosophical Investigations* (Oxford: Basil Blackwell, 1958).

2 Ludwig Wittgenstein, *Zettel* (Berkeley and Los Angeles: University of California Press, 1970), p. 42.

underlying psychological process; a certain kind of face expression offers an exhaustive portrayal of the emotion; or better, it *is* this emotion. The actor knows the emotions felt by the character he interprets to the precise extent to which he is able to represent them for the spectators. Wittgenstein extends this provision, which is the cornerstone of theatre, to every human animal. In his view, a man at the mercy of sadness or wonder does not know the feeling that pervades him any more than what he could communicate about it to a friend by means of a well-calibrated blend of discourses and actions: 'I give myself an exhibition of something only *in the same way* as I give one to other people.'³ Resorting to non-observable mental states in order to explain the meaning of statements and the motivations of silent behaviours becomes necessary if, and only if, we wrongfully separate statements from behaviours—with regard to theatre, if, and only if, the two preparatory stages of a performance (movements on stage without lines, and then the other way round, lines without movements on stage) are not superseded by the restored combination of saying and doing. The evident interweaving of linguistic and non-linguistic activities throws light on the individual outcomes of both. Gestures elucidate words; words illustrate gestures: 'We really shall be explaining words by a gesture, and a gesture by words.'⁴ The invisible is the miserable consolation prize for those who ignore or misunderstand the visible.

It is well known that Stanislavsky obliged his actors to repeat 'good evening' dozens of times, always conferring on this trite phrase different semantic and pragmatic undertones. It is equally well known that, according to Wittgenstein, one and the same question, prayer, and account of an event assume the most various meanings within the countless linguistic performances in which we participate as protagonists or extras. The instructions a director gives to an actor

---

3 Wittgenstein, *Zettel*, p. 116.

4 Wittgenstein, *Zettel*, p. 41.

about the way in which to interpret Othello's grief after Desdemona's murder, or the euphoria of the seducer following an unintended 'yes' are nothing other than Wittgensteinian *Sprachspiele*. In other words, they concern the variable intersection between words and gestures. And vice versa, in describing the *Sprachspiele* inherent to doubt, waiting, and pain, Wittgenstein offers stenographic, yet quite precise, directions to a hypothetical actor. His linguistic performances are full-fledged director's notes.

BIBLIOGRAPHY

ARENDT, Hannah. *The Human Condition*. Chicago: The University of Chicago Press, 1998.

——. 'What Is Freedom?' in *The Portable Hannah Arendt*. New York: Penguin, 2000.

BENJAMIN, Walter. 'Theses on the Philosophy of History' in *Illuminations*. New York: Schocken, 1968.

——. *Selected Writings: Volume 2, Part 2, 1931–1934*. Cambridge, MA: Harvard University Press, 1999.

——. *Selected Writings: Volume 2, Part 1, 1927–1930*. Cambridge MA: Harvard University Press, 2005.

BENVENISTE, Émile. *Problems in General Linguistics*. Miami: Miami University Press, 1971.

BIANCIARDI, Luciano. *It's a Hard Life*. New York: The Viking Press, 1965.

BRECHT, Bertolt. *Brecht on Theatre*. London: Bloomsbury, 2015.

CAVELL, Stanley. *The Claim of Reason: Wittgenstein, Skepticism, Morality, and Tragedy*. Oxford: Oxford University Press, 1999.

FOUCAULT, Michel. *Technologies of the Self: A Seminar with Michel Foucault*. Amherst, MA: The University of Massachusetts Press, 1988.

——. *The Hermeneutics of the Subject: Lectures at the Collège de France 1981–1982*. London: Palgrave Macmillan, 2005.

FREUD, Sigmund. 'The Uncanny' in James Strachey (ed.), *The Standard Edition of the Complete Psychological Works of Sigmund Freud*, VOL. 27. London: Vintage, 2001.

HEGEL, Georg Wilhelm Friedrich. *Aesthetics: Lectures on Fine Art*. Oxford: Oxford University Press, 1975.

——. *The Science of Logic* (George di Giovanni ed. and trans.). Cambridge: Cambridge University Press, 2010.

HEIDEGGER, Martin. *The Fundamental Concept of Metaphysics: World, Finitude, Solitude.* Bloomington: Indiana University Press, 1995.

——. *Being and Time.* Albany: SUNY Press, 2010.

HIRSCHMAN, Albert O. *Exit, Voice and Loyalty.* Cambridge, MA: Harvard University Press, 1970.

HOBBES, Thomas. *De Cive.* Oxford: Oxford University Press, 1983.

——. *On the Citizen.* Cambridge: Cambridge University Press, 1998.

JAKOBSON, Roman. *Il farsi e il disfarsi del linguaggio: Linguaggio infantile e afasia* [The Doing and Undoing of Language. Child Language and Aphasia]. Turin: Einaudi, 1971.

——. *Selected Writings: Volume 2, Word and Language.* The Hague: Mouton, 1971.

KANT, Immanuel. *Critique of Pure Reason.* London: Macmillan, 1929.

——. *Theoretical Philosophy: 1755–1770.* Cambridge: Cambridge University Press, 1992.

——. *Critique of the Power of Judgment.* Cambridge: Cambridge University Press, 2000.

——. *Religion and Rational Theology.* Cambridge: Cambridge University Press, 2001.

——. *Critique of Practical Reason.* Indianapolis: Hackett, 2002.

LEIBNIZ, Gottfried Wilhelm. *New Essays Concerning Human Understanding.* London: Macmillan, 1896.

LEOPARDI, Giacomo. *Zibaldone* (M. Caesar and F. D'Intino eds). New York: Farrar, Strauss and Giroux, 2013.

MANDELSTAM, Osip. *Kamen.* Peterburg: Akme, 1913.

MARX, Karl. *Capital,* VOL. 1. London: Penguin, 1990.

——. *Grundrisse* (Martin Nicolaus trans.). Available at: https://bit.ly/3PVJKyp (last accessed: 1 June 2022).

MERLEAU-PONTY, Maurice. *The Visible and the Invisible.* Evanston, IL: Northwestern University Press, 1969.

PLESSNER, Helmuth. *Laughing and Crying. A Study of the Limits of Human Behavior*. Evanston, IL: Northwestern University Press, 1970.

QUINE, Willard V.O. 'Reference and Modality' in *From a Logical Point of View*. Cambridge, MA: Harvard University Press, 1961.

SCHILLER, Friedrich. *Of the Sublime* (William F. Wertz trans.). Washington: Schiller Institute, 2001. Available at: https://bit.ly/3987O0i (last accessed 1 June 2022).

SCHMITT, Carl. *Der Begriff des Politischen: Text vom 1932 mit einem Vorwort und drei Corollarien*. Berlin: Dunker & Humblot, 1963.

———. *Political Theology: Four Chapters on the Concept of Sovereignty*. Cambridge, MA: MIT Press, 1985.

———. *Theory of the Partisan*. New York: Telos Press, 2007.

SOHN-RETHEL, Alfred. *Geistige und körperliche Arbeit*. Frankfurt: Suhrkamp, 1970.

SPINOZA, Baruch. 'Theologico-Political Treatise' in *The Chief Works of Benedict de Spinoza*, VOL. 1. New York: Dover, 1951.

STANISLAVSKY, Konstantin. *An Actor's Work on a Role*. London: Routledge, 2010.

VIRNO, Paolo. *Parole con parole: Poteri e limiti del linguaggio* [Words with Words: Powers and Limits of Language]. Rome: Donzelli, 1995.

———. *Convention and Materialism: Uniqueness without Aura*. Cambridge, MA: MIT Press, 2021.

WITTGENSTEIN, Ludwig. *Philosophical Investigations*. Oxford: Basil Blackwell, 1958.

———. 'A Lecture on Ethics'. *The Philosophical Review* 74 (1) (1965): 3–12.

———. *Zettel*. Berkeley and Los Angeles: University of California Press, 1970.

———. *Philosophical Grammar*. Berkeley and Los Angeles: University of California Press, 1974.

———. *Wittgenstein and the Vienna Circle: Conversations Recorded by Friedrich Waismann* (Brian McGuinnes ed.). Oxford: Blackwell, 1979.

———. *Tractatus Logico-Philosophicus*. Abingdon: Routledge, 2010.

———. *Lecture on Ethics*. Chichester: Wiley Blackwell, 2014.